60 - MINUTE WINE EXPERT

TASTE WINE THE MASTER'S WAY

A crash course through the basics
of wine and wine tasting
by
RANDA WARREN
Master Sommelier
Certified Wine Educator
Diploma of Wine and Spirits (WSET)

60-MINUTE WINE EXPERT
TASTE WINE THE MASTER'S WAY

An original publication of TOTAL PUBLISHING AND MEDIA.
This work has never before appeared in book form.

TOTAL PUBLISHING AND MEDIA
9731 East 54th Street, Tulsa, OK 74146
www.totalpublishingandmedia.com

Cover and photo credits:
Timothy Lange, ThinAirCreative, Inc.
Broken Arrow Ok

Printed in the United States of America.

FIRST EDITION

DEDICATION

*I dedicate this book to my family for their tireless
support during the ten years I spent
studying about wine and taking
the many examinations.*

*The times I had my nose in a book
or a wine glass, took time away from
being with you, the ones I love most.*

ACKNOWLEDGEMENTS

I want to thank my daughter Brittlyn Bravo – my sunshine. I cannot imagine life without you. To family and friends who supported me and my efforts to succeed on my arduous wine journey, I extend a most sincere thank you.

Thank you to my fellow Master Somms whom I cherish as a second family, and my dear friend and best study partner in the world, Laura Williamson. Laura spent hundreds of hours with me as we dissected wines, tested each other on theory questions and traveled around the country practicing blind wine tasting with Master Sommeliers.

Thank you to Wayne Belding and Sally Mohr in Boulder, Colorado for endlessly making time to construct wine-tastings for me. You had words of encouragement and many useful, sometimes harsh criticisms which ultimately helped me become a Master Sommelier. Many thanks to Doug Frost, MS, MW and Tim Gaiser MS who were always within reach to help me with tasting exercises. Finally, to my fellow Master Somms whom I cherish as a second family. Santé!

A special thank you to my editor, Shirley Hall, of ShirleyHallPoet, LLC, my graphic designer Tim Lange, of ThinAirCreative, and my publisher, Peter Biadasz of Total Publishing and Media for your contributions to this book.

WHAT PEOPLE ARE SAYING ABOUT
60-MINUTE WINE EXPERT

"Randa has an incredible talent when it comes to teaching people about wine and I am thrilled she has transferred her wine knowledge and witty sense of humor to print. She has conducted numerous wine dinners for our Arizona, Oklahoma, New Mexico and California Merrill Lynch clients and the events are always an outstanding success. Her book is an absolute must for anyone looking to expand their wine knowledge in social or business settings."

– Stephanie Bruce - Assistant Vice President, Market Executive Assistant Merrill Lynch Phoenix, Arizona

"I have been interested in learning more about wine and Randa's book nails it! Her approach is simple, easy to understand and remember. Not only is her expertise evident, but what she successfully conveys fits into an enjoyable and fun read. She offers valuable, user-friendly tips for daily wine consumption. Who knew you could put ice cubes in your wine and get away with it? I highly recommend this book to anyone wanting to learn the basics of wine and improve upon what they already know."

– Heather Ezell - Owner, Hang Zen

"I am always entertaining clients over dinner for McGraw Realtors and half the time don't have any idea what wine to order or what to say about the wine. When I found this book, I hit the lottery. My self-confidence around wine has tripled."

– Helen Howard - McGraw Realtors.

"My company based in London, requires me to extensively travel abroad and here in the US. I am always in situations with high-level execs at dinners or business meetings with wine involved. I knew a little about wine but Randa's book took my knowledge to a whole new level. I loved her many jokes throughout the book."

– Luc Tomasino - International Media Executive, London

"As a musician, I am constantly around wine at night but haven't taken much time to learn about it. Give me a Cabernet and I'm happy. When I ran across the 60-minute Wine Expert book, I thought it would be a great shortcut to learn more about wine. It's a super-easy read and I can't believe how much I learned so quickly. Thank you Randa for sharing your knowledge.

Your book rocks."

– Chris Riley - Riley

TABLE OF CONTENTS

CHAPTER	PAGE

FOREWORD

In the most modest of ways I was one of those people who pretended to know how to order a bottle of wine. I never imagined one day meeting someone who would leave me questioning every choice I had ever made.

Two years ago, I met Randa Warren, an, inspiring, charismatic Master Sommelier. I could tell immediately knowing her was going to be an experience unlike any other and ordering, buying, serving and tasting wine would be far beyond inspiring..

Randa Warren grew up in Oklahoma. She graduated from the University of Oklahoma with a degree in Advertising and Journalism and obtained an Associate degree in French at Tulsa Community College.

Currently she is one of only 249 professionals worldwide who have achieved Master Sommelier and one of only 25 women in the world who have this distinction. A Certified Wine Educator and recipient of a WSET Level 4 Diploma from the Wine and Spirit Education Trust, Randa, teaches wine classes in Tulsa Oklahoma, speaks nationwide on how to become a 60-Minute Wine Expert, is a business owner, entrepreneur and contributes to a local publication.

Randa's journey to Master Sommelier is an inspiring story of passion, dedication, hard work and an "I will not quit" attitude. In *60-Minute Wine Expert* she beautifully details the obstacles she overcame, and the wisdom gained as she pursued her passion and now lives her dream.

Sharing wisdom of "all things wine" in this beautifully written, simple, yet professional approach to understanding the basics of wine and wine tasting, Randa speaks to the connoisseur, the restaurateur, and to people like me.

The portrait of her journey, the challenges she faced, and lessons learned makes the contents of this book a must read for wine lovers worldwide. After meeting Randa and reading this book I agree: "Everyone should be able to order, serve and appreciate a good bottle of wine."

– Shirley Howard Hall, Author

INTRODUCTION

I am often asked why I got into the study of wine. My reply is simple; I was tired of being embarrassed at restaurants when trying to order wine. I decided the time had come to learn how to navigate a wine list, order a decent bottle of wine and know a little about what I was tasting.

To make a long story short, I was fed up with spending $40-$60 on a bottle (back in 1995) of Cabernet Sauvignon the server or store employee recommended which ended up being too young to drink, lacking fruit, tasting bitter and tannic – and expensive! 25 years ago, I didn't think there would be much to learning a little bit about wine and how to taste it.

Surely, with a little knowledge I could branch out and start trying new wines. I decided to take a few wine classes and see if I could learn some of the basics. The bottom line is I absolutely hated feeling inferior on a weekly basis when it came to ordering wine and talking about it. I felt it was time to do something about it.

In the 1990's local wine classes in Tulsa were not available. Determined to pursue what was fast becoming a passion, I contacted the WSET, Wine and Spirit Education Trust in New York City and immediately began their three-year home study course. At the same time, I took a Certified Wine Educator preparatory course through the Society of Wine Educators and became a Certified Wine Educator of which there are around 425 in the world.

Because I am so frequently asked, I will share with you what the actual Master Sommelier exam consists of, my journey and what it takes to accomplish it. At the Master level, you must already have taken the Introductory Sommelier level course / exam and have passed the Certified Sommelier and Advanced Sommelier level exams.

There are three different parts to the Master Sommelier exam which is now given twice a year. It consists of Theory, Tasting and restaurant service – called the 'Practical' exam. You must pass all three parts of the exam within a three-year period. If you fail, you must start over and retake all the parts you passed and the parts you failed. Many candidates get completely exhausted and frustrated at this point, give up and quit the MS program.

The Theory exam consists of oral questions – they can ask anything in the world about wine and spirits. The Tasting exam consists of multiple wines you must taste and analyze in 25 minutes. The Practical exam is conducted in a restaurant setting where you perform restaurant service duties while answering theory questions.

The first year I took the exam – and mind you, the exam was only given once a year back in 2003, I passed only the Theory portion. The second year I passed no parts and was devastated. The third year I passed the notoriously difficult Tasting exam but yet again failed the Practical exam – this was the hardest part of the test to pass for me. I started all over the following year and sat for all three parts of the exam again.

I was completely deflated and sickened at the idea of beginning the exam process all over, however, I have pretty thick and calloused skin. I analyzed where I most needed to focus and stomped on the pedal full speed. On an average, I studied theory, practiced restaurant service and blind tasted wine for ten plus hours a day.

On my fourth attempt one year later, I passed both the Tasting and Theory parts of the exam and finally, in the fifth year of taking this monster of an exam, I passed the Practical exam. Whew! Yippee! Thank God! March 22, 2007 was the happiest day of my life! Having successfully passed the Tasting portion of the Master Sommelier exam two times in a row, gave me added insight into the superior skills needed to be a great wine taster. This is what I hope to pass on in writing this book.

Passing all levels of the WSET I made life more frenetic with my discovery of the Court of Master Sommeliers' programs. Started in England with its first exam in 1969, by 1977 the Court of Master Sommeliers was established as the premier examining body of Sommeliers worldwide. I promptly embarked on a journey with this organization which led me through an eight-year marathon of study and testing. Successfully completing all three levels in 2007, I became the 16th woman in the world to become a Master Sommelier.

The study of wine has immensely enriched my life. It has allowed me to not just drink wine to relieve my daily stress, but to appreciate what is in every bottle of wine on my table. I think of all the vineyard workers who grew the grapes and took daily care of them; of the grape pickers standing on their feet 12 hours a day and then transporting their baskets to the winery and much more, all so the resulting wine will taste the best it can.

I also consider the many expenses the winemaker incurred just to get his wine ready for market – not forgetting the history behind a winery and the generations of family involved in building and maintaining the brand of the wine. There is love in every bottle of wine and it's passed on to us once we pop that cork and the memories that follow from glass to mind.

I have been asked hundreds of times what my favorite wine is. My answer begins with a series of questions, 'Who am I with, where am I, what am I eating, and who is paying the bill?' Once answered I can begin to narrow down this answer. In truth my favorite wine changes on a daily basis.

60-MINUTE WINE EXPERT

In the *60-Minute Wine Expert,* my intention is to quickly elevate you to a person with sharper wine tasting skills, a broader understanding of food and wine pairing and someone who can successfully stand up to snooty wine snobs.

I wrote the book with the desire to help people with an interest in wine focus on the philosophy, style, uses and characteristics of wine. *60-Minute Wine Expert* includes:

> ❥ Entertaining with wine.

> ❥ Expanding your knowledge of wine tasting – evaluate/analyze/ examine like a polished wine taster.

> ❥ What millennials just starting to drink wine should know.

> ❥ Sources for expanding your knowledge of wine.

> ❥ How to have better food and wine experiences.

> ❥ What to do when you are handed a wine list.

> ❥ What to do in wine country – visiting wineries.

> ❥ Starting a small wine cellar in your home.

> ❥ The benefits of being able to talk about wine and accurately describe what you are smelling and tasting.

Enjoying wine isn't limited to bottles of wines with corks. It is a passion which can equally include the enjoyment of wines in a box, wines with screwcaps or wines served with ice cubes on a patio in summer months. Wine is for everyone, every day and in every way you chose to consume it.

Allow me to bring a little expertise and professionalism into your life when it comes to a fascinating beverage which reaches back to the beginning of time.

Join me in tasting wine the Master's way.

Chapter 1

THE 60-MINUTE WINE EXPERT'S
PLAN OF ATTACK

This book is designed to give you a quick look at the world of wine, highlighting the most important things you need to know to be a 60-minute wine expert. You will transform yourself from a complete beginner to a person with a solid working knowledge of wine and tasting wine. If you have been a wine lover for a while, you will pick up a lot of useful information to further enhance your enjoyment and hone your tasting skills.

Before you can launch your attack you need to know what wine is and how it's made. Grapes are normally picked in a vineyard in the Northern Hemisphere in September (in April in the Southern Hemisphere).

1

Grapes are brought into the winery in clusters after being picked by hand – or by machine with their stems and leaves still intact. Once in the winery machines called de-stemmers remove the stems and leaves.

White grapes are then quickly crushed in a machine called a press; this machine presses the grapes to release their juices. The juice is then quickly transferred to large tanks or vats for it to settle. It is here the sediment falls to the bottom of the tank. The juice is moved to another tank leaving the sediment behind. This process is referred to as racking.

Red grapes are handled in much the same way, however, the juice which is pressed out of the grapes will rest for a period of time in direct contact with the red grape skins (called maceration). This process which takes from a few days to a week will pull color from the skins – hence giving red wine its depth of hue.

Thick grape skins like the Cabernet Sauvignon grape will end up giving the final red wine a deeper color, and thin skins like the Pinot Noir grape will end up giving the red wine a much lighter color. Rosé or blush wines, as they are often called, are wines which came in contact with the red grape skins for approximately 12-48 hours giving the wine a pinkish color.

To make wine you must ferment the grape juice. Yeast is an organism which exists naturally in the vineyards and on grape skins. Fermentation can occur naturally using yeast on the grape skins and in the air, but most often, cultured yeast is added to the tank holding the grapes to assist in consuming the sugars in the grape. The yeast consumes the sugar in the grape juice and turns it into alcohol and carbon dioxide. This process is called fermentation – and necessary for alcohol to be present in wine.

At some point in future wine discussions with friends, you may be asked about 'organic' wines. Very simply, for a wine to be called organic, grapes must be farmed organically. This means chemicals are not used in the vineyard. These wines are regulated by the government, carry a USDA organic seal and are made without the addition of sulfites. It's important to note that all wines have natural sulfites and are never completely sulfite free.

Along these same lines you should also be aware of the term 'biody-namic' wines. This is a stricter way of farming grapes and built on the writings and philosophies of Rudolf Steiner. He considered the vineyard as one ecosystem and based this system of growing grapes around astrology and lunar cycles. The 'biodynamic' certification is not overseen by the government but by the Demeter Association.

The next 13 chapters will explain where grapes are grown, what major grapes you need to initially know and how to taste wine the Master's way. You will also discover elementary, yet essential knowledge about serving wine, wine etiquette, proper wine temperatures, decanting wine and more.

This useful information is designed to quickly and efficiently get you up to speed with all aspects of wine and enable you to hold your own with friends, peers and anyone you might encounter on the wine tast-ing trail. There will no longer be a need to shy away from intelligently talking about wine in social or business settings.

A great starting word to learn to say properly is *'Sommelier'*

(SOM - like TOM) (UL- rhymes with wool)
(YAH - rhymes with ray). Som-ul-yah.

This is a person who guides you at restaurants; matching wine choices and food pairings to the wines you have chosen.

"I love wine. It's the only reason I get up in the afternoon"

– Anonymous

3

Chapter 2:

MOST IMPORTANT GRAPE VARIETIES AND QUICK FOOD PAIRINGS

OLD WORLD WINES - When you hear this term it refers to European wines or wines produced in western Europe. Europe has been making wine for a longer period of time than the rest of the world – dating back to Roman times.

The most important old-world wines include wines from: France, Italy, Spain, Portugal and Germany. These generally have aromas and tastes which remind you of something earthy. It could be the smell and taste of wet stones, freshly-tilled soil like clay or compost, mushrooms, truffles, forest floor, underbrush or even manure. Old world wines also have lower alcohol and higher acidity due to the grapes often being grown in COOLER climates.

NEW WORLD WINES are wines produced outside Europe. One of the most popular new world wine producing areas is the United States – including areas in California, Washington and Oregon as well as many other states which make wine in smaller quantities.

New world wine areas also include: Canada, Chile, Argentina, Australia, New Zealand and South Africa. Wines from these countries will often smell and taste richer and fruitier.* New world wines are often opposite of old world wines in the sense that they **will smell and taste more like fruit and less like earth and often have higher alcohol and lower acid due the warmer climate.**

Think 'fruit' for new world wines and 'earth' for old world wines. Commit this train of thought to memory.

*There are exceptions to every rule and sometimes we will see an old-world wine which is rich and fruity, possibly the result of a very warm vintage, or a new world wine with earth-like flavors reminiscent of soil and stones.

THE FOUR MOST IMPORTANT WHITE GRAPES:

CHARDONNAY (SHARD-uh-nah):
This grape is best known as coming from Burgundy, France and California. Often called 'Chard', this is one of the most favored white grape varietals in the world and makes an outstanding dry white wine.

Warmer climate Chardonnay (making rich, fruit-driven Chards with higher levels of alcohol and lower acidity) come from California, Washington, Australia, New Zealand, Chile and South Africa. Chardonnay is a white wine with a pale to medium yellow color. The acidity is generally medium or less, which makes Chardonnay have a heavier feeling in the mouth.

Fruit smells and tastes will be reminiscent of ripe apple, lemon, pear and often notes of pineapple and melon. Non-fruit identifiers might include brioche bread or toast, butterscotch or buttery characteristics (from malolactic fermentation explained on page 30) and baking spices like nutmeg, cinnamon, allspice, ginger and vanilla from aging the wine in French oak barrels.

Cooler-climate French Chardonnay is highly sought after among wine enthusiasts. The most prominent area Chardonnay is grown is in the Burgundy area of France. In fact, the most expensive Chardonnay in the world comes from here and is called 'Montrachet' from the appellation of Montrachet.

Other Chardonnays found in Burgundy, but far less expensive than Montrachet, are found in the communes of Puligny (POO-leen-yee)-Montrachet, Chassagne (Chah-SON-yah)-Montrachet, Meursault (MARE-so), Chablis (CHAB-lee) located in cooler northern Burgundy and the warmer Macon area in southern Burgundy including Pouilly-Fuissé (POO-yee/Fwee-say).

French Chardonnay coming from a cooler climate will display tarter fruits including green apple, pear and lemon flavors and aromas. A lovely mineral characteristic holding the wine together reminds one of wet stones or flint.

Quick Food Pairings: Fish including halibut, grouper, sea bass, mussels, clams, shrimp, crab, lobster, sole, scallops, fettuccine cream pasta, popcorn (if the chard is buttery in flavor), cheese, grilled veggies, white pizza, chicken, avocado. Lobster, if grilled, use a Chard aged in an oak barrel (look on the wine label on the back of the bottle).

SAUVIGNON BLANC (SAHV-veen-yone / Blonk):
The most important areas growing Sauvignon Blanc (SB) are California, the Loire Valley, France and New Zealand. In the Loire Valley (Luh-wire), the SB's will have more earth flavor in the form of minerality (wet stone and flint characteristics) than the slightly softer, less-intense versions we find in new world areas like California.

Sauv Blanc as we Masters call it, is intense when smelling and tasting it. You don't have to struggle to smell and taste what's in the glass —it has very vibrant, zesty, zingy aromas and flavors … they simply clobber you head on! SB makes a very dry wine with high acidity which will make your mouth salivate and water much like a lemon does.

SB's are seldom aged in oak barrels so don't expect all the baking-spice flavors we find with many Chardonnays. However, there is an exception in the Bordeaux area of France where SB is blended with Sémillon (SAY-mee-yohn) and often aged in French oak barrels. However, this is not the norm for SB. Most winemakers make the wine in a style which is fresh, clean, zesty and very pure – not encumbered and bogged down by oak (wood) flavors.

Fruit springs out of the glass with strong notes of grapefruit, lime zest, lemon, passion fruit, gooseberry (a fruit popular in England) and tart green apple. SB has non-fruit characteristics of grassiness, jalapeño pepper and what I liken to pungency – the pungency that reminds me of a cat box or cat urine. Yikes! It isn't a very flattering thing to say about SB, but I think you will easily remember this grape by my association of the cat box with grapefruit juice splattered all over —trust me.

Quick Food Pairings: Due to the high acid in this SB, pair it with salads with vinaigrette, goat cheese, chicken piccata, chicken with capers, asparagus soup, artichokes and seafoods like: oysters, mussels, clams, shrimp, tilapia, sea bass, halibut, salmon, tomatoes and pasta with tomato sauce.

PINOT GRIGIO (PEE-noh GREE-gee-oh):
Pinot Grigio (PG) is primarily grown in northern Italy, Alsace, France, California and Oregon. It is usually a dry wine but in Alsace, France we see it made in styles including off-dry (slightly sweet) to very sweet dessert wines with lots of sweetness.

PG is a weaker link in our white wine line-up in the sense Pinot Grigio (PG) is a fairly neutral grape, making light simple wines with flavors and aromas of apple, lemon and pear and hints of nuttiness, especially from the cool climate of North Italy where it is so well known and liked.

It is not aged in oak barrels to keep its simplicity and freshness in-tact. In Alsace, France and Oregon, PG is referred to as Pinot Gris and is the exact same grape as Pinot Grigio. In both of these areas, the PG is richer, higher in alcohol and fuller in body due to the warmer climate the grapes are grown in.

Quick Food Pairings: Burrata (fresh mozzarella) cheese and lighter appetizers like calamari and salami including prosciutto and salami, chicken, a whole gamut of seafoods including oysters, mussels, clams, shrimp, trout, salmon, veggies, a multitude of pastas and risottos, choucroute, Asian-influenced foods and quail.

RIESLING (REE-sling):
Many Master Sommeliers consider this their favorite white wine. It is loved by many chefs and sommeliers around the world due to the high, teeth-grinding acid in the wine which pairs so well with multiple cuisines around the world.

Riesling grows in cooler climates and is best known in Germany in the old world – abundantly from the German areas of Mosel, Rheinhessen (RINE-hessen) and Rheingau (RINE-gow ... as in owl). It has very high acidity. This component in the wine allows it to work beautifully when pairing with food.

Think of Riesling with its high acidity as a squeeze of lemon you might add to food to make the food 'pop' with accentuated flavor. For instance, if you would normally squeeze lemon on a piece of salmon, the Riesling can work as your squeeze of lemon because of its similar acidity with the lemon.

In the new world, we see Riesling grown in the United States mainly in Washington state and New York (Finger Lakes). Fine examples are also grown in new world South Australia (Clare Valley), Alsace, and some stunning examples coming from the Wachau (VAH-cow) area of Austria.

The grape itself has flavors of ripe apple, candied lemon, pineapple, melon and can have a slight petrol smell reminiscent of gasoline but not in an offensive way. This smell and taste is from a chemical compound called TDN (Trimethyl-dihydronaphthalene). This unusual smell adds to the complexity and beauty of the wine.

Riesling comes in styles from dry to sweet although most people associate Riesling with being sweet. Shock your dinner companions by ordering dry Riesling (noted by the word 'Trocken' on a German wine label. Elsewhere in the world you may or may not find the word 'dry' on the label) and everyone at the table will marvel at your wine savvy!

> **Food Tip:** *If I said all food goes with Riesling, would you believe me? Here is a food and wine pairing trick to make any wine go with any food: Add a squeeze of lemon and sprinkle of sea salt to the food you are wanting to pair your wine with, then taste the wine. You will find the salt and lemon known as 'food enhancers' will soften and slightly sweeten the wine and allow it to better pair with the food.*

DO THIS EXPERIMENT:

First: Put a little lemon on the back of your hand and add a sprinkle of salt on top.

Second: Take a taste of dry Riesling or any dry wine.

Third: Lick the area on your hand which has the lemon and salt.

Fourth: Taste the wine again. You'll find the wine becomes softer and sweeter (and better tasting) after the lick of lemon and salt Remember the acid in food diminishes acid in wine making it taste softer.

Quick Food Pairings: Pair sweeter Rieslings (most coming from Germany), with spicy foods including Thai, Mexican, Indian, wasabibased sushi.

It also pairs well with foie gras and other country patés or rillettes, as well as desserts including apples, lemons and pineapples, cheesecake and creme brulée.

The sweetness of the wine will counter the spiciness in the food. The sweetness of the wine will also counter the richness of appetizers like foie gras/paté and match up perfectly with the sweetness the desserts.

Wine and Food Pairing Tip: *You always want the wine to be sweeter than the dessert!*

Pair dry Riesling (called 'Trocken' on German wine labels) with chicken, pork, seafood and shellfish, ham with fruit sauces, duck, lemongrass, sushi, smoked or cured meats, salads with vinaigrettes.

Other White Grapes to Explore: Chenin Blanc from France and the USA, Albariño from Spain, Gewürtraminer from Alsace, France, Moscato (or Muscat) from Italy, California, Australia and southern France, Gruner Veltliner from Austria, Viognier from France and California, Torrontés from Argentina, Vermentino, Orvieto and Verdicchio from Italy.

THE FOUR MOST IMPORTANT RED GRAPES:

PINOT NOIR (PEE-noh NWAHR):
Widely grown in the California areas of Sonoma and Russian River, Pinot Noir from this area is bursting with flavors of bing cherry, ripe raspberry, cranberry, coca cola, beets, herbal notes and spice like clove and nutmeg. It is the main red grape of the Burgundy area where flavors of sour Morello cherry, cranberry and unripe raspberry are more abundant along with distinct earthy characteristics.

New Zealand, Oregon, Chile and southern Australia also produce Pinot Noir. Note all Pinot Noirs are very light in color – this is due to the fact the grape has a very thin skin, therefore not a lot of color to lend to the resulting wines. Learning to recognize Pinot Noirs by their very light color just as you will want to recognize Cab Sauvs by their very dark color (thick skins).

French oak is lightly used when making more expensive Pinot Noirs from California and France. The very subtle taste on the palate allows the bright fruit of the grape to come out in the wines. Remember: Pinot Noir: light color/light tannin and lots of tart red fruits.

CABERNET SAUVIGNON (CAB-ber-nay /SAHV-een-yohn):
The world's best Cabs come from Napa Valley, California and the Bordeaux (BOR-doe) region of southwest France. Other excellent Cabs come from Washington state, Chile, Argentina, Southern Australia and Tuscany, Italy,

Cabernet is king! Remember this by saying 'Cabs have abs' (abdominal muscles). They are usually full-bodied, heavy on the palate and have fruit flavors of blackcurrant, blackberry, black plum and blueberry. Many Cabs, especially those from the Bordeaux region of France, will have additional aromas and flavors of gravel, tobacco and cedar that's associated with spicy oak flavors in the wine.

When French oak is used, Cab often has the taste and smell of baking spices like cinnamon, nutmeg, clove and allspice. Australian Cabs, as well as Cabs grown in cooler areas can pick up aromas and flavors of eucalyptus, mint and green bell pepper.

Because some Cabs are tannic and hard to drink when they are young, we sometimes see Merlot and other wines mixed in to soften them. Tannins found in Cabernet wine come from its thick grape skin but also derive from oak barrels the wine is aged in. When the wine is in your mouth, you will experience a drying sensation which feels like sandpaper on the top of your tongue. Or perhaps, imagine licking a Harris-tweed jacket and that fuzzy feeling you would feel on your tongue. *Yuck!*

Cabernet Sauvignon wines have a dark color to them – quite opposite of Pinot Noir described above. This is due to the thick skin of the grape and adds more tannin to its wines.

Quick Food Pairings: Beef, particular grilled beef, to compliment the oak flavors on the wine. Lamb, game, elk, duck, portobello mushrooms for vegetarians, stinky cheese like Roquefort, Stilton or blue cheese, chocolate, hamburgers, rabbit, sausage and squab.

MERLOT (MARE-low):
This grape makes a much softer style of wine than Cabernet Sauvignon. Merlot grows all over the world and often very close to the same areas where Cabernet Sauvignon is grown. Merlot makes an excellent wine as 100 percent Merlot, but also makes terrific wines when blended into Cabernet Sauvignon and other wines. The Merlot adds body and complexity to these blends.

As I mentioned previously under the Cabernet Sauvignon grape description, by blending the softer Merlot wine into a Cabernet wine, the resulting wine will taste much smoother. Bordeaux, France is well known for their Cab / Merlot / Cabernet Franc / Malbec / Petite Verdot blends we refer to as 'Bordeaux blends' everywhere outside Bordeaux.

Aromas and flavors found in Merlot include blackberry, black cherry, blueberry, red fruit like red cherry and plum and we often can detect a slight green stem-like character (like the stem of a plant) in the wine. Sometimes green bell pepper smells and flavors in Merlot are evident.

Quick Food Pairings: Grilled/roasted beef and prime rib, filet mignon, duck, pork, lamb particularly grilled or roasted, stinky cheese like blue, braised meats, grilled chicken and mushroom dishes.

SYRAH (SEE-rah):

The most important grape-growing places for Syrah are the Rhone valley, France south of the Burgundy area and the Languedoc-Roussillon (LONG-dock/ROOSE-ee-yon) area west of Provence, France. Other areas include Australia, where the grape is called Shiraz (SHE-razz), the United States, Washington state, California, South Africa, Chile and Argentina. Syrah and Shiraz are the same grape.

The fruit you smell and taste from Syrah wine include blackberry, black cherry, blackcurrant and plums. It is important to take note that you will be reminded of flavors and aromas of spiciness from black pepper plus smokiness, herbs, and perhaps a little rubber tire and bacon fat. Syrah loves to be blended with the grapes Grenache and Mourvèdre making smooth, delicious wines.

Quick Food Pairings: Barbecue! pork ribs, brisket, pulled pork, pork roast, and smoked or grilled chicken. Duck with cherry sauce, grilled or braised lamb, mushroom risotto or stuffed portobello, beef kabobs, venison, squab, sushi grade tuna grilled or raw, sausage/brats, grilled salmon brushed with BBQ sauce.

FOUR MORE RED GRAPES TO BE FAMILIAR WITH:

ZINFANDEL (ZIN-fun-del):
Sometimes this red California grape can be confused with Syrah due to its similar spiciness. Let's explore red Zin's most common characteristics. Look for explosive, jammy, rich ripe red and black fruit like red and black cherries, blackberries, red cranberries and strawberry jam. High alcohol normally tags along with red Zin —often over 14% so you will feel a burn going down the back of your throat. The wines can be very intense, rich, jammy and powerful due to the high alcohol.

In making white Zinfandel, winemakers will soak red Zinfandel grapes before fermentation for a very short period of time (12-24 hours) pulling a tiny bit of color out of the red grape skins. This results in blush or rosé-colored wine popular in California.

MALBEC (MAWL-beck):
This is Argentina's predominant red grape from Mendoza but is also grown in southwest France, the United States, Chile, Australia and other areas. It is often blended with Cabernet, Cabernet Franc and Merlot in Bordeaux as well as these other areas just mentioned. It tastes and smells of black and red fruit like plums, spice and has a soft feel in the mouth due to supple tannins. There is a wide range of Malbec styles in Argentina from inexpensive, good value wines to some blockbuster, very full-bodied expressions of the grape.

SANGIOVESE (SAN-gee-oh-VAY-zee):
You must be familiar with this Italian grape as it is the fundamental red grape in Tuscany and more specifically, in Chianti. Known for its high acid, it makes your mouth salivate much like sucking on a lemon. Think of 'lemon meets cherry' — meaning high acid joins up with cherry flavors. This is the perfect wine for many Italian food dishes especially those containing high acid like Marinara and Bolognese-sauced pastas.

Dishes with tomatoes with high acid, and most pasta dishes will go beautifully with Sangio as we fondly call it in the wine world. You'll be reminded of herbs like sage and oregano plus cranberry, raspberry and plum flavors with this wine. It is the red grape of the Tuscan areas of Chianti, Vino Nobile de Montepulciano, Brunello de Montalcino and Montepulciano d'Abruzzo from south of Tuscany.

TEMPRANILLO (TEMP-ruh-NEE-yoh):
This is Spain's most widely-grown red grape and the primary grape of the Rioja (REE-oh-hah) area in northern Spain. If you are going to be familiar with one grape from Spain, this is the one to know.

You will smell and taste red and black fruits in Tempranillo wines and be reminded of a dustiness in the wines. I refer to this 'dustiness' as something 'rustic'. Sometimes iodine and dill will come to mind when tasting them. What is important and unusual in Spain with this wine is it is often aged in AMERICAN oak barrels which give it a taste and smell of planks of freshly sawn 2"x 4" wood, dill and coconut.

HOW TO OPEN A BOTTLE OF WINE

Since you will be opening wine bottles for the wine tasting exercises coming up and beyond, let's discuss the proper way to open a bottle of wine.

I like to use a simple, inexpensive tool called a waiter's key. Most sommeliers at restaurants use this opener. There is a small knife attached at one end which you will need to pull out. Right below the top of the wine bottle, there is a protruding glass lip. Use the knife to make a cut through the foil all around the bottom of this lip in a full circle. Make sure to go completely around this lip 360 degrees making a clean cut into the foil.

Now, use the knife to cut upwards from your cut circle around the lip and use the tip of the knife to cut up the side of the foil on the bottle and then over the top of the bottle through the foil. Wedge the knife under the foil cut and pull the foil capsule off. Fold the knife part back up and now, pull the worm out. This is the curly, auger-looking part of the corkscrew.

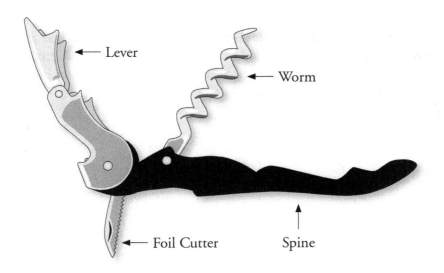

You will need to insert the pointed tip of the worm into the center of the exposed cork. Wind the corkscrew down into the cork 2-3 full turns. You will notice a double-hinged arm or lever that folds out away from the corkscrew across from the knife.

With the worm inserted into the cork, put the bottom part of this movable lever on top of the bottle's opening's edge and secure it with one of your hands so it doesn't slip off the bottle. With your hand still securing the lever onto the top of the bottle, in an upward motion lift the spine or main body of the corkscrew with your free hand.

The cork will begin to come up out of the bottle. Now wind the worm another 2-3 full turns more deeply into the cork and repeat the movement with the hinged lever secured with one hand and lifting the corkscrew's spine upward. The cork should now pull out.

"The only time I ever said no to a glass of wine was when I misunderstood the question!"

– Anonymous

I asked the sommelier at a local restaurant in Tulsa to describe a wine to me he thought I should order. He sarcastically said, "It's a full-bodied wine with nuances of turbulence, moral outrage and complete debauchery. I said, *"Bring it on!"*

Chapter 3

HOW TO TASTE WINE THE MASTER'S WAY™

This is the most important chapter in the entire book. Tasting wine as an experienced wine taster takes a number of years to perfect – yet tasting wine the correct way won't take long to master once you commit this chapter to memory and start practicing.

Make a photo copy of the following tasting sheets and carry them with you until you have them committed to memory. They have everything you need to know to taste wine the Master's way.

Pages 20 and 21 contain a short, condensed look at the steps for analyzing wine and can be used to flag your memory once you have memorized pages 22-26. Pages 22-26 explain in detail all the steps listed on pages 20 and 21.

WINE TASTING QUICK ANALYSIS SHEET

1. The Visual of the Wine:

❯ Is the wine bright and clear?

❯ Variation of color from core color to the outer rim?

❯ Color of the wine?

❯ Bubbles present?

❯ Is the wine viscous?

2. The Smell of the Wine:

❯ Is the wine clean?

❯ How intense is it?

❯ Fruit aromas? List three.

❯ Earth aromas present?

❯ Oak-aging aromas present?

❯ Non-fruit aromas?

❯ Alcohol - feeling of warmth in nose?

❯ Complexity - a lot going on in the wine or not?

3. **The Taste of the Wine:**

- Sweetness level?
- Body?
- Fruit?
- Earth?
- Oak aging tastes?
- Non-fruit flavors?

- Acidity?
- Tannin?
- Alcohol?
- Complexity?
- Finish/length-lingering taste?
- Is the wine balanced?

4. **Initial Thoughts as to What the Wine Is:**

- Old world or new world?
- Cool or warm climate?
- Possible countries the wine could be from?
- Possible grape varieties the wine might be?
- How old is the wine?

5. **What Exactly is the Wine?**

- Country the wine is from?
- From what region?
- Exact year the wine was produced?

WINE TASTING ANALYSIS SHEET – DETAILED BREAKDOWN

THE VISUAL OF THE WINE:

> **Brightness** - Is the wine bright or very bright?

> **Clarity** - Is it clear/cloudy/contain floating particles?

> **Rim variation** - Does the color change from the center of the wine or its core to the outer rim after you've tilted your glass at a 45-degree angle away from you with a white background like a piece of paper behind the glass?

> **Color of the wine** - Whites from youngest and lightest to darkest and showing more age: platinum/straw, light yellow, medium yellow, dark yellow, golden, golden with hints of brown. Reds from youngest and darker to having less color: Black/purple, red, ruby, garnet, mahogany.

> **Viscosity** - This is sometimes referred to as 'legs' on side of a glass above the wine after you swirl the wine in the glass. Legs are a combination of glycerol and alcohol-surface tension. If these legs or droplets are 'slow to form and slow to fall down the side of the glass' this is a sign of high alcohol (over 14% abv = alcohol by volume). If they fall down the side of the glass very quickly, then the wine may have lower alcohol (under 12% abv) as with a sweet German Riesling or other dessert wine?

> **Do you see bubbles in the wine?** - This indicates a sparkling wine like Champagne.

THE SMELL OF THE WINE:

⧩ Is the wine clean?

⧩ Intensity: - What is the intensity of smell - low, medium or high? Does it smell strong or weak?

⧩ Fruit - (Stewed, dried, fresh, baked, bruised). Think of three fruits the wine smells like. Do they remind you of red or black fruit or both?

⧩ Earth - Do you smell anything that reminds you of the earth like soil, minerals, compost, grassiness, wet rocks, truffles, mushrooms, barnyard or manure smells, tree bark, wet cement after a rain storm?

⧩ Wood - Do you smell oak aging (nutty, smoky, caramel-like, mocha, dill, lumber, baking spices like cinnamon, nutmeg, allspice, vanilla or clove)?

⧩ Non-fruit aromas - Flowers / spices / leather / herbs / petrol / gasoline (Riesling wines) / pungent cat urine (Sauvignon Blanc wines) / botrytis (smells like honey aromas) that orginates from a good kind of rot we see some on grapes intended to be dessert wines.

⧩ Alcohol - Do you feel a slight burn, or warmth, in your nose when you smell the wine? This warmth equates to possible high alcohol in the wine.

⧩ Complexity - In a complex wine, you will perceive multiple aromas or layers of aromas. This could be aromas of fruit + earth + development or maturity in the wine + oak aging smells that remind you of vanilla, freshly-sawn wood, baking spices similar to allspice, nutmeg, clove, cinnamon, ginger, or a wood barrel which has been toasted over flames from fire (what we often refer to as 'toastiness').

THE TASTE OF THE WINE:

- **Sweetness** - Is it dry / off-dry (slightly sweet) / medium sweet / very sweet or luscious?
- **Body/weight** - (feels like skim milk, 1%, or 2% heavy milk in mouth) and this equals light, medium or full body?
- **Fruit** - Confirm as on nose. Think of at least three fruits you can taste. Are you reminded of red or black fruit or both?
- **Earth** - Presence or non-presence and confirm as on the nose. Organic or inorganic earth? Organic = compost, manure, freshly-tilled soil, tree bark, mushrooms and truffles. Inorganic = wet stones or cement.
- **Oak aging** - Confirm as on the nose. Do you taste oak? New or old barrels? Is it French or American oak barrels? French oak barrels smell more of baking spices like: nutmeg, clove, allspice, vanilla, ginger or cinnamon and American oak smells more like 2"x 4" planks of freshly sawn wood, coconut, dill, strong vanilla and often smells stronger than French oak barrels.
- **Non-fruit flavors** - Confirm as on the nose. Do you taste: flowers / spices / leather / herbs or honey (from botrytis)?
- **Acidity** - Is it low, medium, high or crisp? Acidity causes your mouth to salivate or water. Put a drop of lemon on your tongue and feel what it does to your mouth – this is high acidity. Low acidity in a wine as with Gewürztraminer will feel heavy in your mouth and not leave your mouth refreshed after sipping the wine. It's almost a little clunky and cloying in your mouth if it has low acidity.

➢ **Tannin** - Is it low, medium, high? Tannin dries the top of your tongue out with a feeling like sandpaper. To practice this, make a strong cup of tea with three tea bags and take a sip swirling the tea around your mouth. You will feel a fuzziness on the top of your tongue. The more you feel and the worse it feels, the higher the tannin levels in the wine. White wines rarely have tannin. Pinot Noir with its thin skin has low tannin and Cabernet Sauvignon with its thick skin has high tannin. Remember that tannin is a feel.

➢ **Alcohol** - Is it low (under 12% abv or alcohol by volume), medium (12-12.5% abv), or high (over 14% abv)? Alcohol gives you a burn going down the back of your throat. The more of a burn you feel as in the case of a California red Zinfandel, the higher the alcohol. Sweet, white German Rieslings will have low alcohol (8%) to give you a few examples.

➢ **Complexity / depth of flavors?** - Can you taste a lot of things or just a few things? Remember as with the nose, this will be apparent by layers of flavors of fruit, earth, oak aging possible maturity of the wine or…. on the other hand, you may not detect much complexity at all in the case of just smelling fruit and little else.

➢ **Finish or length** - short, medium or long? This is how long you can taste a wine after you swallow the wine. If it is under 3 seconds, it is a short finish like a Pinot Grigio. If it is over 4 seconds, it is a long finish. The longer the finish of the wine, the higher the quality of the wine.

➢ **Balance** - Do all the components in the wine work well with each other? Does the wine taste good? Would you buy it again? Is it worth the price?

INITIAL THOUGHTS ON WHAT THE WINE IS?

New World = non-Europe?

Old World = Europe?

Cool or warm climate?

What country is the wine is from?

What is quality level - low / med / high?

What grape varieties could it be?

Age range - very young at 1-3 years old or older?

WHAT EXACTLY IS THE WINE?

Country wine is from? (ex: France)

What region is it from? - (ex: Burgundy region within France)

Appellation or specific area the wine is from? - (ex: Montrachet within region Burgundy within country France)

Vintage? - (exact year wine produced - ie: 2010)

Further explanation of the steps in the wine tasting analysis process:

1. **Appearance of a white wine:** The appearance of a wine can give you many clues as to what is in your wine glass and this is very useful if you are tasting a wine blind (not knowing what the wine is).

    A. If the white wine has a golden color or deep yellow color, this indicates the wine could be a grape varietal like Chardonnay which tends to be a darker color than say, Pinot Grigio. Order a glass of Kendall Jackson Chardonnay and take note of its color.

B. If the white wine has a dark yellow or golden color, it could also indicate that the wine is an older, more mature white wine. White wines as they get older, develop more color and red wines as they mature, lose color in the form of sediment that falls to the bottom of the bottle or glass.

C. If a white wine has a golden color or marked yellow color, it could indicate it is a wine aged in an oak barrel. Wines aged in oak barrels will often leach or pull color out of the wood and into the wine and can make a wine more yellow/gold.

2. Appearance of a red wine.

A. If the red wine is very dark in color with black and purple tones, it indicates a thicker-skinned grape like Cabernet Sauvignon, Merlot, Petit Sirah, a Cabernet blend, like a Bordeaux blend (that includes: Merlot and Cabernet Franc), or Syrah and red Zinfandel. If a red wine is paler in color, it is usually made from a thin-skinned grape like a Pinot Noir, Grenache or Tempranillo from Spain.

B. If a red wine is very dark and black in color and you can't see through the wine at all, we call it opaque. Additionally, if the red wine is dark in color with black, red and purple colors, it is a sign that the wine is very young, and the grape has a very thick skin. Red wines often start out as dark red or black / purple, then move towards ruby red, then garnet and finally, mahogany as they mature and get older.

***** If a wine, red or white is very brilliant with light bouncing off it, it could mean the wine was fined and filtered in the winemaking process to give it a very clean look. If the wine is slightly cloudy, this could mean there was no fining and filtering, OR the wine is spoiled. You will know by tasting it. If it tastes like vinegar, wet cardboard or smelly gym socks, then it is a faulted wine and should be refused and be sent back at a restaurant or returned to a store where bought.

3. **Nose/aromas of a wine:** This is the most important part of the wine tasting process because you can smell over 10,000 different smells compared to your taste senses that includes five senses – sweet, sour, bitter, salty and savory. Spend an adequate amount of time analyzing the nose of a wine as it holds many clues for you when figuring out what wine is in the wine glass when tasting it blind.

4. **Taste/palate of a wine:** You can taste five basic tastes – sweet, sour, salty, bitter and savory or something we call umami (ew-MOMMY). A few examples of foods high in umami are: mushrooms, tomatoes, parmesan cheese and anchovies. Umami is a Japanese word and originates from glutamates and other amino acids. Obviously, taste is the fun part of the process, but honestly, you are really just confirming everything you just deciphered on the nose of the wine.

"I feel sorry for people who don't drink. When they get up in the morning, that's the best they are going to feel all day."

– Dean Martin

Have you ever gotten into a rut drinking a type or brand of wine so often you start to tire of it and it begins to taste blah? I like to say wines like this are a little congressional in their predictability. *Don't let it happen to you.*

Chapter 4

PRACTICE TASTING OF A WHITE AND RED WINE

B elow is a practice tasting example of a white wine and a red wine which can be purchased almost everywhere in the USA at grocery or liquor stores.

Instructions: Buy a bottle of **Kendal Jackson VR (Vintner's Reserve) Chardonnay** from California from the grocery store or liquor store. Chill it until cold.

Now… let's taste a wine the Master's way to give you the flow of how a blind wine tasting should unfold.

WHITE WINE PRACTICE TASTING:

Hold the wineglass by the stem and tilt it away from you at a 45-degree angle with a piece of white paper behind the glass on a table. Make sure you have good lighting in the room.

1. **Appearance/sight** - This has a medium-yellow color fading to a watery rim when tilting the glass at a 45-degree angle with a white sheet of paper behind the wine. It is a clean, clear, bright white wine with no signs of bubbles. The viscosity or 'legs' falling down the side of the wineglass are medium plus or slightly heavy looking.

   This means the droplets of wine falling down the side of the glass above the wine (after you have swirled the wine in the glass) have some noticeable thickness to them and indicates an alcohol level around 13- 13.5% which is medium plus. Legs are just a clue as to what the alcohol levels may be and it's not exact by any means.

2. **Nose/aromas** - On the nose, this is a clean wine with intense fruit smells of baked apple, ripe pear and lemon with some tropical fruits of pineapple and melon. There is a subtle smell of a sweet, white flower similar to honeysuckle. There is nothing earthy in this wine confirming it's from the new world. I also smell a buttery note on the wine. This butter smell is a result of malolactic fermentation which is a secondary fermentation the winemaker intentionally allowed the wine to experience.

   Simply, 'malo' is the conversion of harsh malic acid in the wine, similar to what is found in green apples, to the softer lactic acid similar to what is found in milk. All red wines go through 'malo' as they call it but very few white wines are put through it with the exception of Chardonnay. Winemakers love to put Chardonnay through malo as it rounds out the wine by softening it by reducing its acidity and gives it the buttery smell.

You will smell French (and a little American) oak on the wine indicated by aromas of slight toastiness or toasted oak-like character, caramel and nutmeg (baking spice). The wine is complex because I smell more than just fruit; I smell French and American oak, and a little honeysuckle floral character plus the buttery notes from the malolactic fermentation.

3. **Taste/palate** - On the palate, this is a dry wine. Sweetness in a wine is detected in different parts of the mouth. Normally, I detect it most on the tip of my tongue. If I'm not sure if a wine is dry or has some sweetness, I will stick the tip of my tongue into the wine. I then remove my tongue from the wine and if I don't taste anything on the tip, it confirms the wine is dry.

With sweetness in a wine, you will taste and feel something on the tip of your tongue. To experience sweetness on your tongue with a wine, practice by tasting a sweet Port wine. You will notice a heavy feeling/sweet taste on the tip of your tongue.

Fruit is confirmed as to what we found on the nose; sweet, baked apple, ripe pear and lemon plus pineapple and melon. There is nothing earthy on the wine, confirming it comes from the new world. As on the nose, I detect baking spices and freshly-cut wood indicating the use of French and American oak in the aging of this wine.

The acid in the wine is medium and there is no tannin in the wine. Generally, white wines do not have tannin in them. The complexity is high and the finish/length of the wine after I swallow is over four seconds, so I consider it a long finish – remembering this 'the longer the finish, the higher the quality of wine'. The wine is balanced between the fruit, acidity, oak nuances and the subtle butter flavors.

4. **Initial thoughts on what this wine is:** this is a wine from the new world due to the rich, ripe fruit flavors and lack of earthy smells. This is from a warm climate due to the higher alcohol and medium acidity. The quality of the wine is high due to the complexity in the wine between the expressive fruit, baking spices from the French oak aging, floral notes and balance. Possible grape varietals include Chardonnay or possibly Viognier or Sémillon.

5. **What exactly is this wine?** This is a good quality Chardonnay from the USA, from California- the 2016 vintage.

"This wine is so good, it reminds me of memories I don't even have."

– Anonymous

RED WINE PRACTICE TASTING:

Buy a bottle of Joel Gott California Cabernet Sauvignon from your liquor or grocery store.

Hold the wineglass by the stem and tilt the glass away from you at a 45-degree angle with a piece of white paper behind the glass on a table. Make sure you have bright lighting in the room.

1. **Appearance/sight** - This has a dark purple/red color at the center of the wine tilting the glass and a white piece of paper behind the wine fading to a pale purple rim. There are no signs of bubbles. The viscosity or 'legs' falling down the side of the wineglass above the wine are medium plus.

    As mentioned with our white wine above, this means the droplets of wine falling down the side of the glass above the wine (after you have swirled the wine in the glass) have some noticeable thickness to them and indicates a high alcohol level around 14%. Legs are just a clue as to what the alcohol levels may be and it's not exact by any means.

2. **Nose/aromas** - This is an intense wine on the nose with pronounced aromas of black fruit like black currant, black cherry and black plums. Non-fruit aromas are a hint of tobacco, cocoa and baking spices like all-spice, vanilla and cinnamon from the French oak used in aging the wine.

    There is a slight hint of wet soil or earthiness even though this is a new world wine. New world wines can exhibit earthiness but what we generally see is that the fruit aromas/flavors in the wine are much more dominant in these wines than the earthy characteristics. There is slightly warm feeling I get in the nose of this wine telling me the alcohol could be high.

3. **Taste/palate** - On the palate, this is a dry wine. To confirm this, I stick the tip of my tongue in the wine. When I pull my tongue out of the wine, I don't taste any sweetness on the tip of my tongue which is where you detect sweetness in the mouth. Sweetness is detected on the tip of your tongue – so when a wine is dry you will not taste or feel anything on the tip of your tongue. With sweetness in a wine, you will taste and feel something on the tip of your tongue.

Fruit is confirmed as to what we found on the nose; the black fruits of black currant, black cherry and black plum. There is a hint of earthiness coming through in the form of wet soil but the fruit impressions I get are much, much stronger than the slight earthy taste and this confirms the wine comes from the new world.

I confirm what I smelled on nose with the baking spices of allspice, cinnamon, vanilla along with a wood/oak smell indicating the use of French oak in the aging of this wine.

The acid on the wine is medium and the tannin is medium plus giving the top of my tongue a scratchy feeling of sandpaper. The complexity is high and the finish or length of the wine after I swallow lasts for over four seconds – so I consider it to be a long finish. It's important to commit to memory; 'the longer the finish, the higher the quality of wine'. The wine is balanced between fruit, acid, tannins and the flavors of oak aging.

4. **Initial thoughts on what this wine is?** This is a wine from the new world due to the rich, ripe fruit and higher alcohol and medium acidity. The quality of the wine is high due to the complexity in the wine between the expressive fruit, slight earthiness and baking spices from the French oak aging.

   Possible grape varietals this could be include Cabernet Sauvignon, Merlot and a 'Bordeaux blend' that is a combination of grapes often blended together in Bordeaux that include Cabernet Sauvignon, Merlot, Cabernet Franc, Malbec and Petit Verdot.

5. **What exactly is this wine?** This is a good quality Cabernet Sauvignon from California, Napa Valley, 2014 vintage.

"I had a recent physical with my doctor and he told me I need to watch my drinking. I now try to sit at a bar with a mirror across from me."

– Anonymous

Chapter 5

FOUR BEGINNING WINE TASTING COMPARISON EXERCISES

I want to give you some introductory wine tasting exercises to help you improve your wine-tasting skills. This will help you learn to distinguish between a few major grape varietals. It's easy and fun! Try to get wines which are in the same price range. I recommend wines in the $15-$20 range. Buy some decent wine glasses from Pottery Barn or better yet, some crystal-tasting glasses from Riedel (rhymes with needle) – the Vinum model or the Spiegelau brand. You can order these online.

Taste the wines in a well-lit room with a white sheet of paper under the glasses to see the color in the wines.

Use the tasting analysis sheets on pages 22-26 to guide you through the tasting.

WHITE WINE COMPARISON EXERCISES:

1. **Chardonnay wine versus Sauvignon Blanc.** These are two of the most important white grapes and taste quite different from one another. Buy a bottle of each and chill them down. Practice tasting them side by side for at least three days in a row or more. Pour three ounces of each wine in separate, wine-tasting glasses.

Note the color differences - the Chardonnay is darker and the Sauvignon Blanc lighter with some green reflections in the wine. Smell and taste each wine and note the Chardonnay smells and tastes more like apples and pears and the Sauvignon smells and tastes more like grapefruit and lemon.

The Chardonnay has a butter-like smell and taste from malolactic fermentation and also tastes and smells like baking spices and wood from French oak where the Sauvignon Blanc smells and tastes like cut grass and is very pungent reminding one of a cat box or cat urine.

The acid on these wines are very different from one another. The Chardonnay has only medium acid that makes your mouth salivate a little bit and the Sauvignon Blanc has HIGH acid that makes your mouth water a lot (like squeezing a lemon in your mouth).

Finally, tape a post-it note or label under each glass identifying the wines, so you can't see the writing from above and mix up the glasses. Taste the wines again without knowing which wine which is. See if you can tell which one is the Chardonnay and which one is the Sauvignon Blanc. Practice this 'blind' tasting test between the wines until you can tell the difference in the wines.

2. **Dry Riesling wine from old world Europe versus an Italian Pinot Grigio from old world Europe.** Choose a Riesling like Dr Loosen Red Slate German dry Riesling and an Italian Pinot Grigio like Santa Margarita. Chill both wines and pour three ounces of each wine into separate tasting glasses.

The Riesling is a little more yellow in color. The Riesling will smell and taste more intense (stronger) and have more tropical fruit smells and tastes reminiscent of pineapple and melon plus baked apples and pears. You may also notice the Riesling has a distinct smell and taste of gasoline or what we sometimes call petrol. Don't be worried if you don't identify this right away – it will come in time. The Pinot Grigio will smell and taste subtler, with notes of mild lemon, apple and pear.

The Riesling has very HIGH acidity making your mouth water like crazy and the Pinot Grigio has only medium acidity. Both of these wines are from the old world (Europe) and we can taste a mineral/stone character in each one. The Riesling reminds me of a slate stone and the Pinot Grigio is a little more non-descriptive stone or rock. Neither one of these wines has any oak aging on them, so you will not smell or taste oak at all. The Riesling will have a very long finish of over 4 seconds and the Pinot Grigio will have a short 1-2 second finish.

Now, mix the wines up and taste them 'blind' with labels under the glass so you can't see. How did you do? Keep practicing with these same wines for several days.

Repetition is the key. Do these exercises over and over for several days until you can distinguish between the grapes while tasting blind.

Advanced suggestion: try all four of the wines above together (in separate glasses) blind and notice the differences in each grape. Practice until you can identify each wine correctly from the others.

RED WINE COMPARISON EXERCISES:

3. **Cabernet Sauvignon wine versus Pinot Noir.** Choose a Cabernet like Columbia Crest H3 from Washington state and an old world or European Pinot Noir like Chateau Louis Latour French Bourgogne which is from Burgundy, France. Pour three ounces of each wine in separate wine glasses.

When you look at the two wines side by side you will immediately notice that the Pinot Noir is a much lighter color than the Cabernet. This is because Pinot Noir is a thin-skinned grape and hence delivers a lighter colored wine with lower tannins.

Remember thick-skinned grapes like Cabernet Sauvignon result in darker-colored wines with higher tannin levels. As a side note, darker-colored wines contain more histamines and can give certain people headaches. I have good news for them; ask your doctor about taking an antihistamine like Claritin or Zyrtec after 1pm and then proceed to drink red wine. I'm not a doctor and can't legally prescribe this, but I've heard of people trying it.

The Cabernet smells and tastes more like black fruit – blackcurrant, blackberry, black cherry and the Pinot Noir more like red fruit – red cherry, raspberry and cranberries. The Cabernet has intense fruit smells and tastes and the Pinot is more subtle and delicate.

Note the Cabernet is more fruit like in its taste confirming it is from the new world (everywhere outside of Europe) and the Pinot Noir has earthy smells and tastes of freshly-tilled soil and wet stones confirming it comes from the old-world or Europe. The is a good comparison of an old-world wine versus a new world wine.

When you rinse the Cabernet around in your mouth for three or four seconds, you notice it doesn't make your mouth water much, so, medium acidity. It also leaves a significant drying sensation on the top of your tongue like sandpaper. This is high tannin. In contrast, the Pinot Noir has low tannin as you don't feel much fuzziness or drying on the top of your tongue.

The Pinot also has higher acid than the Cabernet and makes your mouth water more than the Cab. Both wines seem to have the same degree of a finish. After you swallow each wine, you have a lingering taste for about three seconds so medium-quality wines. We remember that the longer the finish, the higher the quality of wine.

4. **Old world Sangiovese wine (from the Chianti area of Tuscany) versus a red Zinfandel wine from California (new world outside of Europe).** Choose a Chianti like Gabbiano Chianti Classico or Ruffino Il Ducale and a red Zinfandel like Seghesio or Rombauer from California.

Note the darker color of the red Zinfandel and the slightly orangish color of the Sangiovese. Most Italian red wines will have a similar color – pale to medium ruby fading to an orangish color on the rim of the wine when you have the glass tilted away from you at a 45-degree angle.

The smell of the red Zinfandel is much more intense than the Sangiovese with red and black fruit smells. It smells and tastes much richer with more fruit on each sip and has only medium acid and high alcohol over 14%. The tannins are soft in the red Zinfandel.

The Sangiovese is more tart with higher acidity and you are reminded of tart red fruit like cranberry, raspberry, pomegranate and red currant. With Italian red wines my friend Doug once told me to remember them by the phrase "lemon meets cherry"; tart cherries join up with sour lemons!

This equates to the fact this wine has high acid. It also has medium-plus tannin and you can definitely feel a scratchy, sandpaper-like feeling on the top of your tongue. You will not taste anything earthy in the red zin but will taste notes of soil and stone in the Sangiovese reminding you of earth. If you are used to drinking only California or new world wines, the Sangiovese may be a little hard to enjoy at first because of its high acidity and sour cherry fruit.

Side note: *After your tasting exercise is completed, pair the Sangiovese (Chianti) with a lovely marinara or Bolognese sauce and pasta. The acid in the wine will cut through the richness of the pasta and work amazingly well with the high acid in the tomatoes. Always pair regional wines with regional foods!*

"I heard recently in the New England Journal of Medicine, they have finally come up with a definition for an alcoholic: a person who drinks slightly more than their doctor!"

– Anonymous

Chapter 6

OVERVIEW OF FOOD AND WINE PAIRING

THE CORRECT ORDER TO SERVE WINE WHEN ENTERTAINING

Pair sparkling wines before still wines, white wines before red wines, dry wines before sweet wines, light wines before heavy wines, young wines before older wines (example: 2015 before 2000), less-complex wines before more-complex wines, cheap wines before expensive wines, and old-world wines (European) before new world wines (non-Europe).

1. **Know the difference between taste, flavor and texture.**

   A. **Taste** - We have five basic taste senses - sweet, sour, bitter, salty and savory or what we call umami. Umami contains glutamate and other amino acids and makes foods taste better. Foods high in umami include parmesan cheese, mushrooms, tomatoes, anchovies and cured meats. If I have a sweet bite of food, I will want to look for a wine with some sweetness like a German Riesling or Moscato to pair with the sweet taste of the food.

   B. **Flavor** - Cherry is a flavor, chocolate is a flavor, and rosemary is a flavor. Flavors are a mixture of taste, smell and texture. If you have a piece of duck breast with a cherry glaze, we see the cherry flavor is playing an important part in this dish. We want to find a red wine with abundant cherry flavors like a Pinot Noir from California or a Grenache from southern France which has lots of cherry flavors to match with this glaze. Sometimes this is called bridging flavors in the wine to flavors in the food.

   C. **Texture** - Texture is how something feels in your mouth related to touch. It could be light, heavy, chewy, crunchy, slimy, oily or rough. If I take a bite of fried chicken, I experience crunchiness and oiliness from the oil the chicken was fried in. I want to find a wine with high acid like Sauvignon Blanc to cut through the oily feeling on my tongue and/or effervescence or bubbles from sparkling wine to cleanse my palate after every bite of this fried chicken.

2. **Traditionalists have always said you have to pair white wine with fish and red wine with meat. It's a good rule but it doesn't work all the time. Let's look at a few pointers to keep in mind.**

   A. **Preparation of the food** - Let's take a raw piece of chicken and steam, poach or boil it. The preparation is pretty simple and dull. Because of this the chicken should be paired with white wine so we don't overpower the simple preparation.

But if we take the same piece of raw chicken, and grill, bake, sauté or broil it, what have we done? We have added some depth of flavor and some caramelization and now, simply because we changed our preparation method, we can serve a light red wine with this piece of chicken.

The point to remember: pair your wine to the preparation not to the protein.

B. **Sauce on food** - Let's take a cooked piece of chicken and add a lemon, caper sauce. The key component is the lemon in the sauce and because it is so light, we should serve a white wine with it. Most white wines have more acid in them than red wines, and if we choose a white wine with high acid to match the high acid in the lemon sauce, we will have a good match between food and wine.

I would choose a wine like Sauvignon Blanc or Riesling for this pairing. We are matching high acid in the wine with high acid in the sauce.

If we take a piece of chicken and add a red wine-mushroom sauce to it, because there is red wine in the sauce, we can actually pair a red wine with the chicken. I would choose a lighter style of red wine like a Pinot Noir, Grenache, or Sangiovese from Italy.

The point to remember: pair your wine to the sauce and not to the protein.

"Wine is the answer! I can't remember the question."

– Anonymous

TEN FOOD AND WINE PAIRING RULES

1. **Use wine to refresh your palate after every bite of food.** High acid wines work best.

2. **Match like with like** - as above, if you have high acid in a food item, find a high acid wine to match the similarity. Goat cheese has high acid and is a great pairing with Sauvignon Blanc's high acid.

3. **With desserts** - sweet nibbles, you always want the wine to be sweeter than the dessert. If you have a piece of sweet wedding cake, the best match will be a sweet Champagne or sparkling wine, not a dry one.

4. **Match the weight of the wine with the weight of the food.** Light, fresh mozzarella cheese will go better with a light Pinot Grigio than with a heavy, full-bodied Chardonnay aged in an oak barrel.

5. **Acid in food will reduce the feeling of acid in wine.** If you squeeze a lemon on the back of your hand, lick it and then taste a Sauvignon Blanc that has high acid, the acid in the wine will seem less and the wine will have a sweeter taste.

6. **Avoid bitter foods like walnuts with bitter wines like some Cabernet Sauvignons or the Nebbiolo grape in Barolo, Italy.**

7. **Salty foods tend to work nicely with sweetness in wines (think of prosciutto and melon) and salty foods work well with acidic wines.**

8. **Spicy food goes best with sweet wine.** The sweet wine neutralizes the spiciness in the food. Spicy food and tannic wines like Cabernet Sauvignon don't work well together. The heat in the food will make the tannin in the wine be more pronounced in your mouth.

9. **Bubbly wine goes well with oily, fried foods like calamari and fried chicken.**

10. Use acid in wines to cut through rich dishes. Think of butter-dipped lobster tails. Instead of a rich, heavy Chardonnay with butter flavors that will compliment the butter sauce for the tails, you might opt for a high acid, dry Riesling to cut through the richness and let the food show off a little.

You have lots of options and remember opposites attract. Sweet Port wine loves to be paired with pungent, salty blue cheese. This match ends with a butterscotch flavor in your mouth and is absolutely divine.

11. Watch out when it comes to artichokes and asparagus when drinking red wine.

Asparagus contains compounds like asparagusic acid and the sulfur-containing compound called methyl mercaptan (contributes to the strong smell in your urine after eating asparagus). The bottom line is asparagus can give red wine and oaky white wines a metallic and unpleasant taste. Worse case take a sip of red wine first, then a bite of asparagus or artichoke!

The best wines to drink with asparagus include citrus-driven, and unoaked wines like: Alsace Riesling and oak-free Chardonnay, but they are terrific with wines like Sauvignon Blanc and Gruner Veltliners with their vegetal or herbal flavors.

Artichokes on the other hand, contain a chemical acid called cynarin (SIGH-nuh-rin) which makes everything taste sweeter and that includes wine. The best wines to drink with them have high acid and very little residual sugar (very dry wines). As with asparagus, Sauvignon Blanc and Gruner Veltliner are excellent, as well as Vinho Verde and Fino Sherry.

QUICK GO-TO FOOD AND WINE PAIRINGS

WHITE WINE PAIRINGS:

1. **Riesling (sweet) or Moscato** with spicy food including wasabi sushi or California rolls.

2. **Sauvignon Blanc** with vinaigrettes, high acid salad dressings, oysters and goat cheese.

3. **Viognier** with almost any cheese or a cheese board.

4. **Chardonnay** with popcorn, lobster, scallops, salmon, halibut, clams, mussels or rich fish.

5. **Pinot Grigio** with Buratta cheese, light pasta or by itself with no food to interfere.

6. **Gruner Veltliner** - Austrian wine with asparagus-based dishes or artichokes.

7. **Albarino** - Spanish wine with paella, tapas like croquetas, frittatas, shellfish, any seafood, ceviche.

8. **Champagne** - with salty caviar, oysters, fried foods, sushi and brie cheese.

RED WINE PAIRINGS:

1. **Pinot Noir** with pepperoni pizza, duck, grilled chicken, salmon, grilled or roast lamb, mushrooms, beets and Camembert cheese.

2. **Merlot and Cabernet Sauvignon** with heavy meats like filet mignon and prime rib, lamb shank, smoked ham, duck confit or grilled duck, cheese like Cheddar, Gouda and Gorgonzola.

3. **Syrah and red Zinfandel** with BBQ foods like spareribs, brisket, pulled pork, venison, duck, lamb, pork belly and sausage.

4. **Sangiovese** (often from Chianti, Italy) and Nebbiolo (from Barolo and Barbaresco, Italy) work well with tomato-based pastas, game, lamb, beef, mushroom and meat risottos, truffle-infused dishes and sausage.

5. **Tempranillo** from Spain with sausage, game, squab, duck, lamb, paella, beef and cheese tapas, Spanish hams like Jamón Serrano and Ibérico, and Manchego cheese.

6. **Malbec -** Beef stew, braised beef, BBQ foods like spareribs, meat loaf, grilled steak, brisket.

7. **Rosé wines -** pizza, charcuterie, antipasti, pork, smoked chicken, liver paté and shrimp.

"My doctor told me to stop having intimate dinners for four people...unless, there are 3 other people."

– Orson Wells

EASY CHEESE AND WINE PAIRINGS

❧ **Blue cheese (Roquefort, Gorgonzola, Danish, Amish, Stilton)** - sweet Port wine, Sauternes, Muscat, Madeira, red Bordeaux wines, Cabernet Sauvignon, red Zinfandel, dry or sweet Sherry, Amarone, and Barolo/Barbaresco from the Nebbiolo grape, and Rhone blends

❧ **Brie** - Red Bordeaux, California Bordeaux blends (Cabernet Sauvignon, Merlot, Cabernet Franc, Petit Verdot), Champagne or sparkling wine

❧ **Camembert** - Champagne, Cabernet or red Bordeaux, Pinot Noir

❧ **Cheddar** - Cabernet Sauvignon, Chardonnay

❧ **Colby** - Chardonnay, Pinot Noir, Viognier

❧ **Comté** - Pinot Noir, sparkling wine

❧ **Feta** - Greek white wines like Assyrtiko or Moscophilero,

❧ **Fontina** - Italian red wines like: Barolo Barbaresco, Chianti, Dolcetto and Barbera

❧ **Goat cheese/Chévre** - Sauvignon Blanc, Riesling, Chenin Blanc and Champagne

❧ **Havarti** - Chardonnay

❧ **Jarlsberg** - Pinot Noir, Grenache, Beaujolais

❧ **Manchego** - Tempranillo, Sherry dry and sweet and Cava sparkling wine

❧ **Mozzarella** - Pinot Grigio, Garganiga (Soave area), Prosecco sparkling wine, Sangiovese (Chianti)

⫸ **Parmesan** - stick mainly with Italian whites and reds like Pinot Grigio, Orvieto, Sangievese (Chianti), Amarone, Barolo/Barbaresco and super Tuscans.

⫸ **Triple cream cheeses (French cheeses with over 60 % butterfat)** - your best bets are red Bordeaux (Cabernet or Merlot based), Champagne and sparkling wine.

"After a particularly bad day, I told my bartender, 'I'd like what that man on the floor was drinking.'"

– Anonymous

Chapter 7

BASICS OF WINE ETIQUETTE

1. **When you are at a winery enjoying a wine tasting** or simply at a wine tasting at your local liquor store or a wine-tasting party, the first thing you need to understand is you shouldn't consume every wine. You need to learn to take a sip of wine, swirl it around in your mouth for 4-5 seconds and then spit it out into a spit bucket or a cup.

Spitting wine out during a tasting of multiple wines is important because you don't want to get plastered in the first 30 minutes of a tasting especially if you are going to be tasting 10-20+ wines. Pace yourself on trips to wine country so you can maximize how many wineries you can visit. Always take notes at your tastings in case your memory fails you after a few glasses of wine.

If you don't see a spit bucket, simply ask for a disposable cup so you can spit into it. Sure, it's okay to drink some of the wines you will be tasting; but get in the habit of spitting most of the wines. Then, at the end of the tasting you can go back and re-taste some of your favorite wines and imbibe a little. Be sure and drink water between each of the wines you taste and/or take nibbles of food.

2. **Tips for navigating a public wine tasting.**

A. Find the wine information sheet that has all the wines listed and prices plus other specifics and a pen to take notes.

B. Take good notes so you remember what you like and don't like.

C. If there is a water pitcher on each table, this is to rinse your glass when switching between white and red wine. I don't find it necessary to rinse glasses with water after each wine I taste. I will rinse my mouth with water occasionally during the tasting or eat bland crackers.

D. Don't congregate too long at each wine station. Taste the wine(s) and take time to visit with the representative pouring the wine for no more than two minutes, then move on to allow others behind you in line to also taste.

E. It's perfectly fine to go back and re-taste your favorites wines. But, don't be a wine hog!

F. If you have time, try to do a little research before you go to the tasting on the wineries or area (say Italy). Have some fun! Don't feel like you have to write every little smell or taste down!

G. Talk about the wines with other people at the tables who are also tasting the wines – you may learn from other tasters and discover points in the wines you missed.

H. Talk to the representatives pouring the wines and ask for additional reading material they may have as handouts. If you particularly like a wine, be sure and ask questions about it – where the grapes were grown, what kind of oak was used in aging the wine, how many cases of the wine were made, does the winery have a high-end reserve wine that you might have a taste of.

3. **What to do when visiting a winery:** When you are going to be in wine country (Napa Valley, California or Tuscany, Italy for example), get on google and research the top wineries in the area and see where you might want to visit. Call ahead and make an appointment for a personal wine tasting or tour of the winery. There is usually a fee for these tastings/tours.

Ask to visit the production area where the wines are made and see where the grapes are grown. Often the tour guide will walk you through the entire process of growing grapes, bringing them into the winery, the fermentation process and allowing you to view the barrel rooms where the wines are stored before they are released.

When you have your wine tasting at the winery, ask if there are any special, more-allocated wines you might taste. Don't forget to 'spit' out your wines as you taste if you are going to be tasting a lot of wines. You don't want to get drunk and embarrass yourself or your friends. Sure, drink some, but pace yourself especially if you are visiting multiple wineries in a day.

If you like some of the wines you sample at the winery, ask about shipping some of the wine home or buying some to put in your suitcase. Southwest Airlines allows you to check two bags and you can always check a styrofoam wine-shipper box as a piece of luggage. Buy a Styrofoam container to put your wines in so they are protected on the airplane. Most wineries sell them.

4. **When you go to someone's home for dinner:** be sure to take a bottle of wine. If the host or hostess decides not to use the wine, leave the wine with them as a gift. Don't insist they serve your wine. It's up to them to decide what wine they are serving with the meal. Before you take a bottle, you could inquire with the host or hostess what food will be served and then decide what bottle you want to bring to compliment the food.

5. **Maneuvering through a wine list at a restaurant for your table:** When ordering the wine for the table, don't order the cheapest bottle on the menu. Choose a wine a few dollars more (like one-third more expensive than the cheapest one) depending on your budget. Look at the wine tastes of those at your table and gauge how much to spend.

 If most of the people don't often drink wine or normally drink cheaper wines, don't spend a bundle on your wines. Order what you think the majority of guests will like. Often, I find I have to order one bottle of white wine and one bottle of red wine, so everyone has what they may like unless you get lucky and everyone wants red wine, or everyone wants white wine. Worse case, there is nothing wrong with ordering wines by the glass of each guest's choice.

"I love having fruit salad for dinner. Ok, ok, it has fermented grapes in it. Alright, the truth is, I am yet again having wine for dinner."

– Anonymous

LEARN HOW TO READ A WINE LABEL

If you look at a bottle of Kim Crawford Signature Reserve Sauvignon Blanc from New Zealand: the front of the label states the name Kim Crawford referring to the producer of the wine. Under that it says 'Signature Reserve' referring to a higher tier of wine than their basic Sauvignon Blanc.

The wine was produced using the winery's best Sauvignon Blanc grapes including grapes grown in the most optimum part of the vineyard. Less of this 'Signature' wine was produced than regular Kim Crawford Sauvignon Blanc, making it more expensive and sought after.

Below you will see the grape's name, Sauvignon Blanc and next to that, the word Marlborough. Marlborough refers to the area in New Zealand the grapes were grown, and the wine was produced.

Some labels may just say 'New Zealand' or 'California' or 'Bordeaux' and not a specific small parcel we call an appellation. This means wines from all over New Zealand or California (etc.) could be blended together to make the wine. If a parcel or appellation is mentioned on the label, then most of the wine in the bottle will be from that specific area. The better wines will generally specify a specific area, like Napa Valley, or Margaux, Bordeaux for example.

On the back label, you will again see the producer's name, a grape name, the area where the grapes were grown, and wine was produced, repeated at the top. Below this, there is a description of the wine followed by website and importing company's information.

Below this you will see a government warning about pregnant women drinking wine. Finally, below the warning, (you will always find the following somewhere on the label) you will see the size of the bottle (750 ml), the alcohol content (12% by volume) and the words 'contains sulfites'.

Sulfites are found in every wine in varying amounts and protect the wine from spoilage. Even organic and biodynamically-produced wines have sulfites despite the words 'no sulfites' on the label. If a wine has less than 10 parts per million sulfites, the label can say 'no sulfites'. They still contain a minute amount of sulfites.

Many people blame headaches they get from wine on sulfites, but more often it can be from the histamines found in tannins from grape skins in red wine. Check with your doctor first, but my remedy for a red wine headache is: TAKE AN ANTIHISTIMINE around 3:00 pm in the afternoon if drinking red wine that evening! And don't forget two Advil before bed. Again, check with your doctor first before doing this as I can't legally prescribe this.

Don't hesitate to ask the sommelier for wine suggestions. The sommelier knows the wine better than anyone in the restaurant. If budget is a concern, simply hold up the wine list to the Somm and discreetly point at a wine in the price category you want and say something like this: "I'm looking for something similar to this". The Somm should pick up on your price point.

> *Suggestion: I find when I'm ordering for a larger group of inexperienced or light drinkers, I generally choose either a California Chardonnay (heavy) or Sauvignon Blanc (light) for whites and, for reds: either California Pinot Noir (light) or Cabernet Sauvignon (heavy).*
>
> *If you are dining in a seafood restaurant, order white wine and at a steak house, order red wine. Make sure guests know they can order wine by the glass. Two sure winners on the pricy side are: 1) For a white wine selection: California's Kendall Jackson VR Chardonnay, La Crema or Sonoma Cutrer Chardonnay or Honig Sauvignon Blanc and for reds: California's Meiomi Pinot Noir or the red blend 'Prisoner' ($$$) are sure winners.*

Feel the bottle of red wine when the server brings it to the table. If it is too warm, ask the server to bring an ice bucket for the red wine and chill it about 10 minutes. This slight chill will make the red wine taste better and reduce the feeling of the alcohol in the wine. It can make a $20 bottle of wine taste like a $40 bottle of wine.

When you taste the bottle of wine the server brings, and you find something unpleasantly wrong with the wine, politely send it back. Ask the sommelier to taste it and he will more than likely agree with you. If the wine tastes like wet cardboard, vinegar or dirty gym socks it is undoubtedly affected by Trichloranisole (shortened to abbreviation TCA) a yeast spoilage.

Many people use the term "this wine is corked" to describe TCA. TCA can originate in a winery from corks, equipment or the environment in a winery and is not a good smell or taste. It won't harm you but be sure not to order the same wine again that night as the entire selection of this wine may be tainted! Order a different wine. This also goes for wines you buy at a liquor store or grocery store. If you detect TCA, take the wine back and get your money back or exchange the wine for a different bottle.

"I've heard there are people who actually drink only one glass of wine instead of a whole bottle. We call them underachievers."

– Anonymous

Chapter 8

RECOMMENDED SERVING TEMPERATURES FOR WINE

W ine simply tastes better when it's served at the right temperature. For a few examples of how temperature can adversely affect a wine, look at a white wine which has been chilled under 45 degrees. The wine will be too cold and the aromas and flavors in the wine will be stunted and barely detectable. If a red wine is served too cold, the same thing happens but it can also make the tannins in the wine seem higher than they are and feel harsh in your mouth. On the flip side, if a wine is served too warm, it can make a wine taste heavy and flabby in your mouth.

I have a general rule of thumb called the 15 - 20 rule. Pull your white wines out of the refrigerator 15 minutes before serving them and put your reds in the refrigerator 20 minutes before serving them. The white wines will have time to warm slightly making the aromas and flavors closer to what the winemaker intended them to be. By slightly chilling your red wine, the alcohol burn will be less apparent in your throat and the fruit in the wine will seem more bright and fresh and taste better than if it is served at room temperature.

I like to tell my wine students you can make a $15 Cabernet Sauvignon taste like a $30 Cabernet by simply chilling it for 15-20 minutes.

If you are in a rush – here is a super easy formula on wine temps:

Wine	Temperature in Fahrenheit
Champagne –	45 degrees
White wines –	55 degrees
Red wines –	65 degrees

MORE SPECIFIC TEMPERATURES:

> **Light white wine temperatures - 45-50 degrees.** If you keep your house super-hot in the winter, drop this to 42 -48 degrees as the wine will quickly warm up in a hot house.

Note: if you have a really expensive white wine, you might want to serve it closer to 53-55 degrees, so the aromas and flavors are as expressive as they can be. Examples include: finer Chardonnays from California or France or white Bordeaux. If you are going to be drinking your white wine outside, you might want to chill it more towards 42-45 degrees as it will warm up quickly outside.

❧ **Heavier, full-bodied white wines - 50-60 degrees.** Examples include Chardonnay, Gewürztraminer and Viognier.

❧ **Champagne or sparkling wines - 42-45 degrees.** I may be different than many Sommeliers, but I like my bubbly very cold. Once it loses a little of its temperature, I find the yeast character in the wine becomes overly noticeable. You may like the character, so adjust to suit your tastes. Never store your Champagne for long periods of time (over 6 months) in the fridge.

❧ **Rosé wines - 47-52 degrees.**

❧ **Light red wines - Particular fruity wines like Beaujolais - 53-55 degrees.**

❧ **Full-bodied, heavier styles of red wine - 60-65 degrees.** Examples include Cabernet Sauvignon and Cabernet blends, Merlot, Syrah and red Zinfandel.

❧ **Port wine: 65 degrees.**

❧ **Dessert white wines: 45 degrees.** Examples include: Tokay, Riesling, Sauternes and Sherry.

"Oh you are in my blood like holy wine
You taste so bitter
And so sweet oh
I could drink a case of you darling and I would
Still be on my feet
Oh I would still be on my feet"

– Joni Mitchell

Wine	Temperature in Fahrenheit
Light white	45-50 degrees
Heavy white	50-60 degrees
Champagne/sparkling	42-45 degrees
Rosé	47-52 degrees
Light red	53-55 degrees
Heavy red	60-65 degrees
Port	65 degrees
Dessert wines	45 degrees
Cognac	Room temp

TEMPERATURE TIPS:

Some people find cold beverages hurt their teeth and prefer wine served at warmer temperatures or room temperature. Do what pleases you or your guests. To give yourself the best education with temperatures – try your wines at different temperatures. Pour two glasses of chilled white wine and put one glass back in the refrigerator for 30 minutes and leave one on the counter for 30 minutes. Try both wines and see what you like best.

Sometimes white or red wine gets too cold while chilling or storing it and you may want to warm it up a little. Simply decant the wine into a decanter or carafe to help it warm to the temperature you want.

If your red wine arrives at your restaurant table at room temperature, simply ask for an ice bucket and put the wine in it for 5 minutes. This will make the red wine taste more refreshing with brighter flavors and honestly, make it taste a little more expensive.

Wine Tip: If you are going to be drinking wine outside in the heat of summer try this tip.

First, you must have some leftover wine to start with. Take your half bottle or however much of leftover wine you have, let's say red Zinfandel for example, and put the leftover wine in an ice cube tray and put in the freezer to freeze.

The next time you have red Zinfandel and are headed outside, get a few of your red Zinfandel ice cubes and throw into your fresh glass of red Zinfandel! Be careful not to throw red Zin cubes into your Cab Sauv – although it might make an interesting new blend!

"I've been having a terrible time lately with NOVINOPHOBIA. This is a fear of running out of wine."

– Anonymous

Chapter 9

WINE GLASSWARE, STORAGE AND WINE BOTTLE SIZES

You can have the best wine in the world, serve it in glass wine glasses versus crystal wine glasses, and minimize some of the great attributes of the wine. Crystal glassware is worth the few extra dollars.

Inexpensive wine glasses made of glass are what you see at Target, Pottery Barn, Crate and Barrel, Costco, World Market, Sam's Club etc. More expensive wine glasses are made from crystal and are less durable but help the wine taste at its best.

Crystal is a little thinner and somewhat abrasive on the inside (although you cannot feel it with your fingers) and tends to grab onto the wine a little better than glass does. This helps open the wine up and taste better. Personally, I have both kinds of wine glasses at my house. Glass wine glasses for my rowdier friends and crystal glasses for my friends who are more knowledgeable about wine.

One standard wine bottle holds 750 ml of wine (same as 25 ounces of wine). This equates to either: four, 6-oz glasses of wine or six, 4-oz glasses of wine etc.

When you pour the wine, pour slowly. As I pour I like to count 'one Mississippi, two Mississippi, three Mississippi, four Mississippi' as I pour to give me a gauge of pouring approximately four ounces in the glass. Each 'Mississippi' you count is about one ounce. You can pour five or six ounces per glass, but I prefer a four-ounce pour.

Try to pour everyone the same amount of wine in each glass. It drives me crazy when waiters at restaurants or hosts at someone's home pours a man more wine than a woman! *Really?*

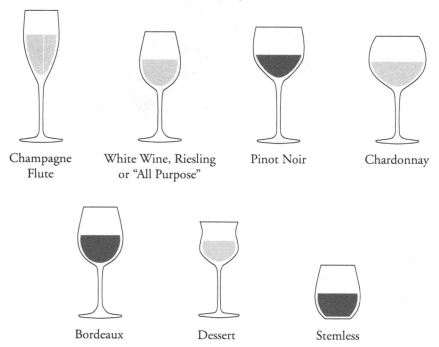

Champagne Flute   White Wine, Riesling or "All Purpose"   Pinot Noir   Chardonnay

Bordeaux   Dessert   Stemless

❧ **Champagne** glasses are usually in a 'flute' shape - tall and skinny and hold 6-10 ounces.

❧ **White wine** generic glasses are smaller than red wine glasses and usually 10 ounces.

❧ **Red wine** generic glasses are larger and usually 12 ounces - more so you have room to swirl.

❧ **Burgundy** glasses are balloon shaped like a big grapefruit and are used for more delicate wines like Pinot Noir because the delicate aromas become more concentrated in the balloon shape, so you can smell the wine more deeply. Often these glasses hold up to 28 ounces but often less.

❧ **Bordeaux** glasses are taller and more slender than Burgundy glasses and designed to serve Cabernet Sauvignon or heavy red wines like Merlot, Syrah, red Zinfandel or Petit Sirah in them. As these wines are more intense, you don't need to capture the aromas as you do with the Burgundy glasses. The aromas have no trouble rushing out of the glass into your nose! These glasses hold up to 28 ounces but often less.

❧ **Port/Sherry/Dessert** glasses are smaller ranging from 4 to 6 ounces.

Smelling Tip: When smelling a wine, stick your nose into the glass and begin to inhale. After a few seconds, open your mouth and breathe through your mouth at the same time. Now exhale through your nose. It's all done in three steps, one right after the other – one leads into the other. Inhale – open mouth, breathe through the mouth – exhale through your nose. This drives all the aromas deep into your retro-nasal cavity, so you get the best, most enhanced smell you can.

WINE STORAGE

> Wine should be stored on its side not standing upright with the exception of Champagne or sparkling wine which can be stored either way – standing upright or on its side.

> Do not store white wines or Champagne in your refrigerator for long periods of time or over six months.

> To store leftover wine in a bottle you haven't finished, you can buy a Vacu Vin Wine Saver ($9) which is a small pump you attach to a rubber stopper (functions like a cork).

Once the pump is attached to the top of your bottle with the leftover wine in it, you then pump air out of the bottle. This helps keep the red wine in fairly good condition for one to two days and white wine for slightly longer.

I love a product called Private Reserve which is a can with inert gas (nitrogen) in it. You spray four squirts into your bottle of wine (that still has some wine in it) and the gas replaces the oxygen in the bottle and preserves the wine for a few days. It won't be 100% but pretty good.

Finally, there is an expensive product called a Coravin which allows you to insert a needle into a cork and remove some wine. It seals the cork so no further air loss occurs. This is great for checking to see how a wine is 'developing' over time and if it is time to drink the wine before it gets too old.

> In general, wine should be stored at 55 degrees and optimally in a temperature-controlled wine refrigerator. This means there is a steady, unfluctuating temperature, where the wine rests with the right amount of humidity (around 70%) so the corks don't dry out over time. White wines are usually kept colder than 55 degrees.

❧ I have some 1995 Bordeaux wines which I recently opened and found the corks had started to dry out. The wines had been stored properly from 1998 when I bought the wines. Because the corks are drying out, I have now added more moisture (bowl of water) in my wine refrigerator.

❧ Sam's Club and Costcos sell small wine-storage refrigerators for several hundred dollars so it won't break your bank account. If you are starting to collect wine, investing in proper storage is quite important. I highly recommend a wine-storage refrigerator. Beyond Sam's Club and Costco, Amazon is a good place to search. I suggest starting with a 50 or 100-bottle refrigerator you can put in your bar or have installed in your kitchen. Then, when the wine bug really bites and you are buying lots of wine, go up to a 300-bottle wine refrigerator etc. We are talking wine refrigerators, not regular kitchen refrigerators.

❧ If you don't have a wine refrigerator for storing wines, be sure to keep wines out of sunlight and warm temperatures. Wines should be stored in a space which doesn't get a lot of vibration and movement, under a stairway for example. Avoid storing wines in your hot kitchen and never on top of your refrigerator or in a garage which gets hot in the summer and cold in the winter. Basements can be a consideration depending on how the temperature fluctuates between seasons.

❧ I used to store wine bottles in my closet behind my clothes so my husband, Stephen, couldn't see them and complain I was spending too much money on wine. Storing wine under a bed in a cool room of the house or apartment is another alternative for those who don't have a wine refrigerator.

❧ Finally, you can rent temperature-controlled storage units in buildings depending on how safe they are and if they are located in a good neighborhood. They may not be humidity controlled but will work fairly well for storage.

WINE BOTTLE SIZES:

› **Topette** - Half-Quarter = 93.5 ml - mostly used for sample bottles.

› **Piccolo or Split** - 187.5 ml (often used for Champagne).

› **Demi-bouteille or half bottle** - 375 ml - or half of a standard 750 ml size.

› **Standard bottle** - 750 ml - Most widely distributed size and equals 25 ounces of wine.

› **Magnum** - 1.5 Liters -equals 2 standard 750 ml bottles.

› **Double Magnum** - 3 Liters -equals 4 standard 750 ml bottles.

› **Jeroboam (non-Champagne)** - 4.5 Liters -equals 6 standard 750 ml bottles.

› **Imperial** - 6 Liters - equals 8 standard 750 ml bottles.

› **Salmanazar** - 9 Liters - equals 12 standard 750 ml bottles.

› **Balthazar** - 12 Liters -equals 16 standard 750 ml bottles.

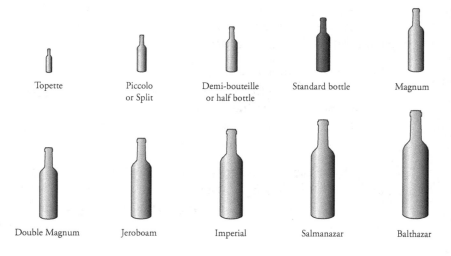

| Topette | Piccolo or Split | Demi-bouteille or half bottle | Standard bottle | Magnum |

| Double Magnum | Jeroboam | Imperial | Salmanazar | Balthazar |

> ❧ **Nebuchadnezzar** - 15 Liters - equals 20 standard 750 ml bottles.
> ❧ **Melchior** - 18 Liters - equals 24 standard 750 ml bottles.
> ❧ **Solomon** - 20 Liters - equals 26 bottles (rare).
> ❧ **Sovereign** - 25 Liters - equals 33.3 bottles (rare).
> ❧ **Primat** - 27 Liters - equals 36 bottles (rare).
> ❧ **Melchizedek** - 30 Liters - equals 40 bottles (rare).

"I started a wine diet ten days ago and am pleased to say I have actually lost three days on this diet!"

– Anonymous

Tip I got from a *New Yorker Magazine* cartoon: If you don't have time to buy a bottle of wine to take to a dinner party, just hand the host $40 when you arrive and say, "This is what we would have spent on a bottle of wine." *It works like a charm!*

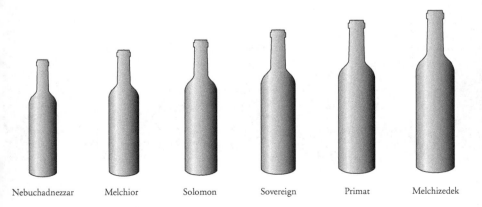

| Nebuchadnezzar | Melchior | Solomon | Sovereign | Primat | Melchizedek |

Chapter 10

CHAMPAGNE: PRODUCTION, PROPER OPENING, SERVING AND BOTTLE SIZES

The good news about Champagne is it is fat-free, gluten free and dairy free making it the perfect beverage for all three meals in a day! (Wine at breakfast is called Champagne!)

My favorite toast about Champagne is one by Madame Lilly Bollinger of the Bollinger Champagne house in Champagne and she said this:

"I only drink Champagne when I'm happy and when I'm sad. Sometimes I drink it when I'm alone. When I have company, I consider it obligatory. I trifle with it when I'm not in a hurry and drink it when I am, otherwise.... I never touch the stuff.... unless I'm thirsty."

I'm pretty thirsty so let's talk about this great bubbling beverage.

CHAMPAGNE PRODUCTION

❧ How is Champagne made? It is really easy and there are three ways: a second fermentation in a bottle, a second fermentation in a tank and simple carbonation.

❧ A second fermentation in a bottle starts out as a still white wine without bubbles. In other words, the winemaker goes through the steps of making a white wine (picking grapes, pressing juice out of grapes and fermenting into a white wine).

❧ Yeast and sugar are then added to the white wine, a cap is placed on the top of the bottle and the second fermentation begins. We call this method 'Method Champenoise' or 'Method Traditional'. It is used all over the world and not confined to just Champagne but other sparkling wines as well.

❧ The fermentation will complete in 10 days to 3 months. Yeast cells begin to die and as the wine matures it will spend a period of time resting on its dead yeast cells. This gives the wine complexity and sometimes a flavor of sour dough bread starter.

❧ Now the dead yeast cells and sediment must be removed in a process called 'remuage'. This is where Champagne bottles are placed in racks called pupitres (wooden racks with holes in it that hold 120 bottles) and manually rotated, turning from horizontal to vertical over several weeks.

❧ This process moves all the dead yeast cells in the wine into the neck of the bottle and forms a plug of goop basically! The other system which rotates bottles mechanically occurs with Gyropalettes. Metal cages which hold 504 bottles, are mainly used for high production sparkling wine like Cava from Spain. This system is much cheaper to perform than the manual system of remuage described above.

❧ Bottles are then put on a conveyer belt and progress into a machine which releases the cap on the bottle. A plug of yeast is released from the bottle by pressure. This is called disgorgement or dégorgement in France.

❧ At this point, sweetness called 'dosage', which is a combination of wine and cane sugar, is added to the bottle to determine how sweet the final Champagne will be. The cork is now added to the bottle and the foil as well and the Champagne is ready to be sent to stores and restaurants.

❧ **From dry to sweet,** champagne labels will display sweetness categories of:

Brut (driest),
Extra-Dry (even sweeter than brut!)
Dry (even sweeter than extra-dry!)
Demi-Sec
Doux (very sweet)

❧ Doux (the very sweetest Champagne and the one best served with desserts or wedding cake!)

❧ If a bubbly is made outside of the Champagne region, it must be called 'sparkling wine'. Another method for making sparkling wine besides Method Traditional, is the tank method or 'Charmat' method.

❧ With the Charmat method, base wine is put in a large tank, then, yeast and sugar are added to the tank and the second fermentation takes place in the tank. The sediment which develops is removed by filtration, sweetness is added, and the wines are bottled. Italian sparkling wine called Prosecco is made in this way. Finally, carbonation is simply where air is injected into a wine to give it its bubbles. This is the cheapest way to make sparkling wine.

Burgundy (wine) makes you think silly things, Bordeaux makes you talk of them and Champagne makes you do them.

– Jean Anthelme Brillat-Savarin

OPENING CHAMPAGNE

>> To open Champagne, pull the little tab sticking out a few inches from the top of the bottle then remove the foil. Or use the knife on your waiter's key wine opener described in Chapter 2a to make a cut in the foil at the base of the cage on your bottle. Make your cut all the way around the bottle in 360 degrees. Use the knife to tear off the upper foil so the cage is exposed.

>> Loosen the wire cage by turning counter clockwise 6 turns and throw it away.

>> Put a towel over the top of the bottle in case the cork flies out prematurely. The pressure in a bottle of Champagne is equal to the pressure in a tire on a double-decker bus! Never point the bottle at someone or have your head above the bottle. If the cork hits you suddenly in the eye, it could blind you.

>> Put one hand (your right hand if you are right-handed) on the bottom of the bottle and the other over the towel with cork underneath keeping a tight grip on the Champagne cork.

>> Slowly turn the bottle at the bottom. Once you feel the cork about to come out of the bottle, take control and go very slowly – try not to let the cork pop and burst out of the bottle. Control it by slightly pushing the cork back into the bottle although you are only slowing the exit of the cork down.

>> Tilt the bottom of the cork slightly as it comes out to let a little air escape. This keeps the loud pop from happening and instead you hear only a slight 'hiss' of air escape the bottle. This hiss should sound like the 'sigh of a contented woman' and not a huge 'pop'! I know this isn't a familiar sound! But hey, it will be soon enough and with some practice.

I only drink Champagne when I'm in love and when I'm not.

– Coco Chanel

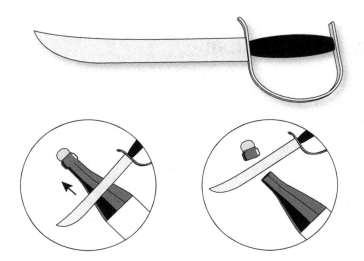

Sabering a bottle of Champagne. This refers to taking the top of the champagne bottle off with a saber sword. The saber looks like a short sword and has a dull blade instead of sharp one. To saber, begin by placing the saber's blade flatly on the side of a Champagne bottle near the base of the bottle with the dull side of the blade pointing towards the top.

Many people use the sharper side of the blade to saber the top off, but I have always used the dull side so splinters of glass don't fly off when the blade hits the lip at the top of the bottle.

Then, move the saber swiftly, and I mean swiftly, up towards the lip of the bottle at the top by the cork keeping the blade flat against the bottle and not an angle. The fast-upward movement actually clips the lip and with the six atmospheres of pressure in the bottle, the fragile top of the bottle with the cork still in it will fly off the bottle! You need to follow through and not stop the movement at the lip. Never put bottles you are going to saber in the freezer first. This will result in it breaking about halfway down and is ugly. Always use caution when sabering as it can be dangerous. Watch a few videos on YouTube to get the hang of it.

Napoleon was a big fan of the saber and said, "In victory I deserve Champagne and in defeat…. I need it."

For purchasing sabers, contact: ranbagel@me.com

SERVING CHAMPAGNE

Make sure the Champagne is chilled to 42-45 degrees.

For optimum chilliness, you can put the Champagne glasses in the fridge before filling them with Champagne.

When pouring Champagne, pour a small sample of wine into the glass and let the foam calm down; then resume pouring very slowly until the glass is 3/4 full. If you pour more than this, the bubbly may end up warming up before you finish drinking the glass. After pouring one or several glasses, be sure and put the bottle back in the fridge or ice bucket. No one enjoys lukewarm Champagne.

Remember not to store your expensive bottles of Champagne in the refrigerator for over 6 months. Simply keep bottles at room temperature in your bar or wine rack either upright or on its side (it doesn't matter which way you store it).

When you think you will be using your bottle, place it in the fridge for two hours, 15-20 minutes in the freezer or 15-20 minutes in an ice bucket filled with ice and water. Alternately, add a cup of salt to the water to speed up the process. Salt melts the ice faster and absorbs heat from the warm bottle you've added to the bucket – and keeps the water extra cold.

| Piccolo | Demi | Standard bottle | Magnum | Jereboam | Rehoboam | Methuselah |

CHAMPAGNE BOTTLE SIZES:

❧ **Piccolo** - 187.5 ml - equals 1/4 standard bottle and 1 glass/wine.

❧ **Demi** - 375 ml - equals 1/2 standard bottle and 2 glasses/wine.

❧ **Standard bottle** - 750 ml - equals 1 standard bottle and 4-6 glasses/wine.

❧ **Magnum** - 1.5 Liters - equals 2 bottles and 8-12 glasses/wine.

❧ **Jereboam** - 3 Liters - equals 4 bottles.

❧ **Rehoboam** - 4.5 Liters - equals 6 bottles.

❧ **Methuselah** - 6 Liters - equals 8 bottles.

❧ **Salmanazar** - 9 Liters - equals 12 bottles.

❧ **Balthazar** - 12 Liters - equals 16 bottles.

❧ **Nebuchadnezzar** - 15 liters - equals 20 bottles.

❧ **Solomon** - 18 Liters - equals 26 bottles (rare).

❧ **Sovereign** - 25 Liters - equals 33.3 bottles (rare).

❧ **Primat** - 27 Liters - equals 36 bottles (rare).

❧ **Melchizedek** - 30 Liters - equals 40 bottles (rare).

Salmanazar   Balthazar   Nebuchadnezzar   Solomon   Sovereign   Primat   Melchizedek

Chapter 11

THE MYSTERY BEHIND DECANTING WINE

A decanter is a glass vessel designed to hold wine which has been poured out of the original bottle. One of my favorites for the money is the Riedel Vivant starting around $25 from Target or elsewhere. It holds one 750-ml bottle of wine which is also equal to 25 ounces of wine. Decanters come in all different styles and sizes. I recommend getting one you are comfortable holding and pouring from.

WHY DECANT?

You can place any wine in a decanter to make it look attractive on a table. The main reasons for decanting are:

> To get oxygen into the wine more quickly than simply removing the cork from a bottle. When a wine aerates as with decanting, it softens up and becomes ready to drink more quickly than without aerating it. If you have a massive, young Cabernet Sauvignon wine like Far Niente from California, this wine will taste smoother and less tannic by exposing it to air through decanting.

> The next reason is to remove sediment from a wine. Older wines develop harmless sediment that can come from yeast cells, particles of grapes and stems, tartrates, and polymers. You'll also see more of this in a wine that has not been filtered or lightly filtered in the winemaking process.

As a wine ages, certain molecules in the wine combine and form tannin polymers which fall out of the wine in the form of sediment. Generally, wines years or older will start to develop sediment yet I have had it in two-year old wine also! Port wine is notorious for having sediment.

When you decant an older wine in preparation of drinking it, first let the wine bottle sit upright for a day or more, or at least a few hours. Then, when ready to start decanting, place a candle on the table and light it.

Open your wine carefully and slowly so the cork doesn't break. (If it does break, use a special tool called an 'Ah-so' which can be purchased at wine stores. It has two prongs which slide down each side of the broken cork in the bottle. You then twist and ease the cork up and out of the bottle). When the cork comes out of the bottle, wipe the top of the bottle with a cloth.

Place the small lit candle on a table underneath the wine bottle's neck as you pour. If right-handed, hold your decanter in your left hand and bottle in your right hand with the candle underneath the neck of the bottle. The candle should be about a foot under the bottle. Don't touch the bottle to the decanter when pouring.

Begin pouring slowly so you can see the wine as it comes through the neck from the light of the candle under the neck. When almost all the wine has been poured from the bottle, you should start to see the sediment enter the neck of the bottle. This is the time to stop pouring the wine, so the sediment doesn't enter the decanter. There should be about a half inch or inch of wine remaining in the bottle. Put the bottle aside. Blow out the candle.

> ❧ Another reason to decant is to warm up a wine which might be too cold.

> ❧ Finally, decanting can be done simply for the drama of it. Show off your wine, decanter and decanting skills!

Wine Bottle Aerators: Another way to aerate a wine is with something you attach to the top of your opened wine bottle called an 'aerater'.

These are great to use with young, big wines like Cabernet Sauvignon, Cab blends like Bordeaux, Barolos and Barbaresco's (acidic and very tannic wines from the Nebbiolo grape), Chianti Classico Riservas, Spanish Rioja Gran Riservas and Super Tuscans. They don't have to be used with just the above-mentioned wines, but most young red wines that are full-bodied.

Chapter 12

WINE EDUCATION – WHAT AND WHERE?

H ere are sources for expanding your wine education:

> Subscribe to *Wine Spectator* magazine: www.winespectator.com. You can buy the monthly magazines at Barnes and Noble or subscribe through the website. They have an awesome app you can pay for monthly and get wine reviews and ratings on your phone.

❧ Read *Wine Advocate, Decanter* magazine, *Wine Enthusiast* and *Food and Wine* magazine. Buy and read books on wine like *Wine for Dummies, Wine Atlas, Wine Bible* and the *Sotheby's Wine Encyclopedia* and Immer's book called *Great Wine Made Simple.*

❧ **Professional wine education:** Start level one with the WSET (Wine and Spirit Education Trust). They have four levels and branches in New York through the International Wine Center and other cities around the United States. Passing all levels of the WSET program are mandatory before entering into the elite, high-level Master of Wine program.

> Telephone: (212) 239-3055
> Website: info@internationalwinecenter.com

❧ Take the **Introductory Master Sommelier 2-day course** given in multiple locations on multiple dates around the country. The course covers the world of wine and spirits and introduces you to blind tasting with 22 wines from major wine areas in the world. Cost is around $525. The next levels of the Master Sommelier program are:

> Certified Sommelier
> Advanced Sommelier
> Master Sommelier
>
> Go to: www.mastersommeliers.org
> (707) 255-5056

❧ Check out the documentary movie *Somm.* It will give you lots of insight into what it takes to become a Master Somm.

❧ Fast track your Sommelier studies at: International Culinary Center in New York and Northern California. www.internationalculinarycenter.com

❧ Check out wine programs offered at the Culinary Institute of America in Napa Valley. www.ciachef.edu

☙ Start a monthly wine tasting group with a group of friends. Tasting with friends and tasting in a blind format where wines are covered with bags will teach you a lot about learning to differentiate between grape varietals.

☙ Join the Society of Wine Educators.

> Website: www.societyofwineeducators.org
> (202) 408-8777.
> This great group has a conference each summer covering all sorts of wine-related topics for members.

> They offer different levels of study programs:

> Certified Specialist of Wine
> Certified Wine Educator
> Hospitality/Beverage Specialist
> Certified Specialist of Spirits
> Certified Spirits Educator

☙ Many local wine stores have wine tastings you can attend. Many restaurants have wine dinners featuring winemakers. This is a great way to meet other wine lovers and the winemaker at the same time.

"I recently had a man come to my liquor store and ask, 'What wine goes best with severance pay?'"

– *New Yorker Magazine* cartoon

"OF COURSE SIZE MATTERS!, someone recently yelled at me. No one wants a small glass of wine!"

– Anonymous

Chapter 13

STARTING YOUR PERSONAL WINE COLLECTION, ONLINE WINE BUYING AND WINE FUTURES

T here is not a lot to starting a wine collection – just interest, stores or sources from which to buy and money. Buy a few wines, find a place to store them, and keep a spreadsheet or diary of what you have.

Many people tell me they can't have wine around the house which they can't drink for a while. I tell people to buy wines to drink (and plenty of them) and buy wines to store – put them in your cellar, wine refrigerator, in a closet or under your bed. Just separate the two – wines for drinking now and stored wines for drinking later. It just requires a small amount of discipline to wait a year or several years until you open the wines.

Research the wines you buy and write down (on your spreadsheet) the recommended age to start drinking the wine – and when the wine should be drunk by. I have a bottle in front of me, Chateau Pavie 2003 Bordeaux from Saint Emillon. It was rated 100 points when it was released and now rated 96 points in 2018. The drinkable age range is 2015 - 2030. I know I should drink this wine before 2030 for it to be at its best.

SUGGESTIONS FOR STARTING A WINE COLLECTION:

❧ Concentrate on buying wines you like, of course, but wines which will age for an extended period of time whether one year or 30 years. For instance, buying rosé wine and most white wines to store for 5 years is a bad idea as the wines will be too mature in just 3-4 years.

❧ Buy wines above $25 from excellent producers who have high ratings from *Wine Spectator* magazine, Robert Parker of the *Wine Advocate, Wine Enthusiast* and *Decanter* magazine like:

- Cabernet Sauvignon or Cab blends focusing on French Bordeaux, California Napa Cab, Washington state Cab

- High-end Chilean/Argentinian Cab or Cab blends,

- Higher-priced Malbecs from Argentina,

- Notable, high-rated Shiraz from Australia

- Expensive Pinot Noir from California or Burgundy

- French dessert wines like Sauternes

- Italian Barolo and Barbaresco

- Italian Chianti Classico Riserva

- Italian Super Tuscan

- Portugal's vintage Port wines (from declared years)

- White French Chardonnay wine from: Burgundy like Montrachet, Puligny and Chassagne Montrachet, Meursault and Chablis

- White Chardonnay, over $30, from California

- White Bordeaux from France over $30

- White dry and sweet Riesling from Germany.

- Vintage (from a particular year) French Champagne

My personal cellar consists of what I like best which is 70% percent red Bordeaux dating back to 1995, 10 percent California Cabernet, 5 per cent Barolo, 5 percent red Burgundy and the rest is German and French Riesling, Austrian Gruner Veltliner and Port wine.

WHERE TO BUY WINES ONLINE

Two stores I buy wines from online who ship to most states are:

Wine Exchange in California at www.winex.com and Kahn's Fine Wines & Spirits in Indianapolis at www.kahnsfinewines.com

WHAT ARE WINE FUTURES?

When Bordeaux, France announces a good year (vintage) many large online stores will offer an opportunity to buy the wine ahead of release – we call this 'futures' buying. This means you can buy wines at 'first tranche' or first opportunity prices which are the lowest prices the wines will be offered and way ahead of when the wines will be sold in retail stores.

These 'first-tranche' offers happen about two years before the wines are sold on retail shelves. When the 'first-tranche' offers are sold, the sellers will then offer 'second-tranche' prices which are a little higher.

First, look for Wine Spectator's and Robert Parker's reviews on these wines then buy as soon as the wines are rated. Prices will gradually go up in the two years before the wines hit the retail markets. For instance, in the fall of 2015 (after the 2015 wines are rated) while they are in barrels by the critics, you can place future orders for these wines even though you won't receive them for several years.

Wine futures can be offered from other areas like Burgundy, France, Italy and California.

Every now and then, wine doesn't sound good and a martini does. Dorothy Parker had this to say, "I like a martini, two at the very most, three and I'm under the table and four, I'm under my host."

Chapter 14

20 MOST-ANSWERED QUESTIONS

1. **Q:** What do you think of wines with screw caps?

    A: Screwcaps are a wonderful way to preserve inexpensive young white and red wine. For long term storage of your better wines, opt for corks. Corks allow a little air to get into the bottle over time and let the wine mature gracefully.

2. **Q:** What's the best way to save leftover wine in bottle?

    A: Use a 'Vacu Vin' wine pump or use Private Reserve Wine Preservation spray which is a can with nitrogen in it that you spray into your wine bottle with leftover wine. Also, with red and white leftover wine, put the bottle in fridge as the colder temps slow down bacterial growth in the wine that makes it taste bad.

3. **Q:** How do you store leftover Champagne?

   A: Crazy but simple is to just put the long part of a spoon down the neck of the wine bottle without letting it touch the wine. That's it. It will keep the bubbles alive for one day, max two. Alternately, you can buy wine stoppers which clamp on to the top of the bottle for around $10.

4. **Q:** Should you chill red wine?

   A: Here is the 15 / 20 rule. Pull your whites out of the fridge 15 minutes before serving so they aren't so cold you can't taste flavors. Reds go into the fridge 20 minutes before serving them. This brightens up the fruit and mutes the alcohol slightly making it taste better.

5. **Q:** How can I make a $10 Cabernet taste like a $30 Cabernet?

   A: Slightly chill the red wine as noted in question number four.

6. **Q:** What's the best temperature to store your wines?

   A: Around 55 degrees at a 70 percent humidity in a wine storage unit and if you have a one-temperature-level in the unit. If you have two (one for white and one for red), keep your reds at 55 degrees and the whites at 45 degrees.

7. **Q:** When do you know when a red wine in your cellar or wine refrigerator is ready to drink?

   A: Generally speaking, red wines over $25 may be drinkable for 5-7 years. More expensive red wines over $30 from areas like Bordeaux and Napa Valley can age over 12 years and often up to 25 years or more. I suggest researching a wine upon purchase and getting a gauge of what sort of life span it may have according to the experts who have tasted it.

Keep a notebook or computer spreadsheet with this information so you have an idea when to drink the wine and when it might start to go downhill. For researching your wine's life span, Google:

Wine Spectator - www.winespectator.com
Vivino - www.vivino.com
Wine Advocate - www.erobertparker.com
Decanter magazine - www.decanter.com

8. Q: How can I avoid getting headaches from red wine?

A: Headaches are often caused by the histamines from the tannins in red wine and not sulfites. Check with your doctor first, but my advice is to take an antihistamine around 3pm in the afternoon and this may allow you to drink red wine that night. Check with your doctor about this before trying it.

9. Q: Do red wines have more sulfites than white wine?

A: No, white wines have more sulfites.

10. Q: Is it okay to put ice cubes in your wine?

A: Generally, not. It's very amateurish to put ice in your wine as it waters it down. But I have a way to do it where it's very beneficial! Any leftover wine you have from a night of drinking, put in an ice cube tray. Remember what the wine was, like red Zinfandel etc. The next time you want to sit outside on a hot evening and drink wine, put some of your red Zin ice cubes in your new glass of red Zin (from new bottle). This is great in hot climates!

11. Q: I have some old bottles of wine I would like to sell. How do I do it?

A: Contact an online wine-auction house like: Acker Merrill, Sotheby's, Christies, Zachys – all with representation in NYC or Wine bid at www.winebid.com. Also, you can look in the classified area in the back of *Wine Spectator* magazine to find names of people who broker the sale of wine.

12. Q: Wines in Europe do not contain sulfites - true or false?

A: False. All wines contain sulfites even those that may say 'sulfite free' on a wine label. Sulfites are naturally present in all wines.

13. Q: How long does it take to chill a bottle of white wine or Champagne?

A: In the fridge for at least 2 hours, freezer for 15-20 minutes, and ice bucket filled with ice, water and salt for 15-20 minutes.

14. Q: What can I use on almost any food to allow me to drink any wine with it?

A: First, add a sprinkle of kosher salt and a squeeze of lemon to any food and then sip the wine. Acid in food diminishes acid in wine.

15. Q: To drink and drive responsibly, how much wine could you consume in an evening?

A: One 4-ounce glass of wine per hour. Not more than 2-3 glasses over the course of an evening. Drink a glass of water after each glass of wine and consume food during the evening.

16. Q: If I see white crystals floating in my wine, should I send it back?

A: No. These are harmless tartrate crystals that usually develop in a wine due to temperature fluctuations during the shipping process.

17. Q: What does a 'bad' wine smell like? Should I send it back?

A: If a wine is infected with TCA (Tricloranisole), it will smell like dirty socks or a wet, moldy basement. It is not harmful, but you should send the wine back at a restaurant or return the bottle to a liquor or grocery store.

18. Q: If I don' have a wine refrigerator, what is the best place to store my wine?

A: Store your wines in a cool, dark part of your house like under a bed or in a closet not exposed to lots of movement.

19. Q: When do you decant a wine?

A: Decant to remove sediment in the bottle with older wines or Port. Decant to add air to a wine to make it taste smoother and drink sooner, to warm up a too-cold wine and finally, for the drama – making an evening more fancy or special and impressing your friends.

20. Q: If I can't afford French Champagne, what is a good alternative?

A: Your best bets are Cava sparkling wine from Spain, Prosecco from Italy and sparkling wine from California or New Mexico.

A FEW FINAL WORDS...

Here is a cool acronym for you to ponder: the word is **TASTE.**
T-A-S-T-E

T - Stands for 'take' your blinders off'. If you are mainly drinking one or two wines like Chardonnay and Cabernet Sauvignon, branch out! Start experimenting more with old world wines like Spain's Tempranillo (Rioja), Italy's Sangiovese (Chianti) and France's Mourvèdre from Bandol. What awaits you will blow you away!

A - Stands for ''accelerate' your wine-tasting skills by starting a wine-tasting group with your friends or colleagues. It's one thing to see the label on a bottle of wine and know what exactly you are drinking. But what if you have a bottle hidden inside a brown paper bag and can't see the label? You taste the wine 'blind' (not knowing what you are drinking) and then use all the skills you picked up in this book to deduce what the heck the wine is. You will get better figuring out what the wines are with practice.

S - Stands for 'savor' everyday smells and tastes you encounter and link them to the wines you are drinking'. For instance, when your lawn is freshly mowed, pick up a clump of grass and smell it. The smell of grass is often found in Sauvignon Blanc. Freshly-cut jalapeño in another smell and taste we are reminded of in Sauvignon Blanc. Smell a freshly-cut Jalapeño pepper as a guide.

Quick clarification - do winemakers put fresh jalapeños and grass in Sauvignon Blanc to give it those smells and tastes? Do they put blackcurrant in Cabernet Sauvignon? NO! These aromas and tastes are coming from the grape itself, the fermentation process, oak barrel smells from aging and the terroir (which is loosely defined as the area around where grapes are grown like the soil, the climate etc).

T - Stands for 'take trips' to wine country. For example, if you are in San Francisco on business or pleasure, take an extra day and drive an hour north to Napa or Sonoma and visit some wineries. Wine tasting and wine education is great fun.... and sometimes a business expense if you can maneuver it! Have Randa Warren take your group on a personalized wine trip to France, South Africa or other areas. www.randawarren.com

E - Stands for 'educate' yourself with wine classes and reading wine magazines like *Wine Spectator* as well as wine books.

You should now have an excellent grasp of tasting wines, food and wine pairing, wine storage, glassware, wine temps, the most important grapes – their origins, and much more. You are now a 60-minute wine expert. Congratulations! Go forth and taste wine the Master's way.

I drink wine to make other people more interesting.
It works every time!

ABOUT THE AUTHOR

Randa was born in Dallas, Texas and grew up in Tulsa, Oklahoma where she currently lives. She graduated from the University of Oklahoma with a degree in Journalism and Advertising. She has an Associate Degree in French from Tulsa Community College. Her daughter, Brittlyn, lives in Dallas, Texas.

In addition to having a passion for wine, Randa is a professional barbecue competitor. She competes in competitions in Oklahoma, Arkansas, Missouri and Kansas. She loves the quote "You don't need no teeth, to eat this meat."

Randa has been a member of the Confrerie du Tastevin in Burgundy, France for over 20 years. She speaks on being a 60-Minute Wine Expert for various organizations and clients around the country, owns a retail wine store in Tulsa, consults for restaurants and gives local wine classes in Tulsa Oklahoma. She takes groups on wine tours around the world.

To contact Randa, go to: www.randawarren.com or email: ranbagel@me.com